T0285588

# Praise for *Go Far, Give Back, Live Greek*

"I have known George for many years and have witnessed firsthand the warmth of his friendship and the strength of his commitment to democracy. *Go Far, Give Back, Live Greek* is a wonderful invitation to see the world through his eyes."

—Massachusetts Governor **Michael Dukakis**

"This compelling memoir is an extraordinary example of the success that is achieved through perseverance, the importance of recognizing the obligation of duty in a democracy, and the power of an indomitable spirit. *Go Far, Give Back, Live Greek* illustrates perfectly how George Danis represents the true meaning of Philotimo."

—**Arthur T. Demoulas,** Food Merchant, Market Basket Supermarkets

"A wonderful book and example for our young generations. A struggle, turned into a challenging adventure, by a young man of strength and character; the cornerstone attributes of what made our America what it is today. I hope many of our young people will read and be inspired by the journey, sacrifices, and determination that seeded the success of Mr. Danis and our great nation, the USA."

—**Dean Metropoulos,** Entrepreneur

"America is a nation of immigrants, from many places but with similar stories. Danis's own story, beautifully told in *Go Far, Give Back, Live Greek*, reminds us of the grit, determination, and kindness that immigrants have brought, generation after generation, and are the bedrock of what is best about our country."

—Massachusetts Governor **Deval Patrick**

"Having known George for many years, I have witnessed his commitment to democracy. *Go Far, Give Back, Live Greek* is a wonderful invitation to the reader to reflect on what it means to be a true citizen of our country through his eyes."

—**Marty Meehan,** President, University of Massachusetts

www.amplifypublishinggroup.com

*Go Far, Give Back, Live Greek: A Memoir*

The views and opinions expressed in this book are solely those of the author. These views and opinions do not necessarily represent those of the publisher or staff. The author has tried to recreate events, locales, and conversations from their memories of them. In order to maintain their anonymity in some instances, the author may have changed the names of individuals and places, and may have changed some identifying characteristics and details such as physical properties, occupations, and places of residence.

**For more information, please contact:**
Amplify Publishing, an imprint of Amplify Publishing Group
620 Herndon Parkway, Suite 220
Herndon, VA 20170
info@mascotbooks.com

Library of Congress Control Number: 2023920716

CPSIA Code: PRV0324A

ISBN-13: 978-1-63755-969-7

Printed in the United States

# GO FAR, GIVE BACK, LIVE GREEK

A MEMOIR

GEORGE E. DANIS

amplify

an imprint of Amplify Publishing Group

# CONTENTS

CONTENTS

**PART TWO**

# WE THE PEOPLE: A LETTER FROM ME TO YOU

WHEN YOU'VE LIVED A LIFE that's been as long and as full as mine, I suppose it's somewhat inevitable that you will end up becoming a storyteller. You look back on your lifetime of experiences—the joyful, the painful, and all the others that cover everything in between—and you feel that you would like to share them with people. You feel that you have something to give back. So from time to time you find yourself sitting around a table in a restaurant or at home, or standing before a small crowd of people at some event or other, talking long into the night as you tell friends and strangers about some of the things that have happened to you along the way.

People will laugh and smile. Sometimes they'll even offer you some advice.

"You should write a book," they say. "These stories are too good not to share."

For the longest time, I always waved away those comments with a smile and a quick change of subject. Eating and talking and laughing with friends is one thing, but a book? It didn't ever feel right to me. I liked telling my stories, but I just didn't have the appetite for putting them in a book—not that there's anything wrong with storybooks, but I always felt that they weren't for me. Maybe it's a legacy from my childhood, maybe it's because of my engineer's mind, but my favorite books are the ones that offer more than a few hours of entertainment or distraction. If I'm going to read a book, I want to get something tangible out of it.

Yet somehow, after years of deflecting these suggestions, I started to wonder. What if I could write something with purpose, something with a tangible benefit? What if I could weave these stories together into something that was more than just whipped cream—something that had substance, that could offer something valuable to the people who read it? If I could pull that off, then maybe a book wasn't such a bad idea after all.

So while I can't tell you precisely when I decided to write this book, I can tell you why.

I don't just want to distract you for a few hours. I don't just want to make you smile. I want to offer you something valuable (at least, I hope this will be valuable to you). I want to give you something that will last, something that, maybe, will help. Because when I look at the world around us today, I think it's in trouble. It's in trouble, and it needs fixing by the only people who can really make a difference—the regular, taxpaying, vote-casting people like you and me.

The citizens.

## Before We Begin . . .

As an engineer I was trained to make things not just practical and functional but also clear and easy to use. I bring that same approach with me to this book, and I want to leave no room for ambiguity or confusion. I want to make sure that you, as you currently hold these pages in your hands, are in no doubt about the message I want you to take away from this.

So . . . in case you're the kind of reader who's a whole lot better at starting books than they are at finishing them, I'm going to give you the essential truth right here at the start, not the stories—you're going to have to do some reading for that—but the message that I think we all need to take on. I'm going to lay it all out for you right now in black and white across a handful of pages. That way, if you don't get beyond the part where my friend has his arm broken by a German soldier, or the bit where I'm busted out of jail by a future president of the United States, or my early days in business when there was so much for me to learn, you'll not leave empty handed.

Sound good?

Good.

So let's begin . . .

## Living Greek

The first thing to know is that the idea of living Greek isn't a matter of how much olive oil you put on your salad or the type of feta cheese you eat. It's about people. Living Greek means learning to see the value of community. It means helping your neighbors, offering your support to people who need it, and realizing the responsibility that lies on us all.

Long before I moved to the United States and ever heard the phrase "we the people," I grew up with a constant and clear illustration of the power of community. Even though it was not a phrase that translated into Greek, "we the people" was one of the cornerstones of Greek society. We had such a strong sense of community, of mutual dependence, of citizenship. When people were in need, we the people helped. When danger threatened our peace, we the people united. Whenever someone was determined to find a route out of poverty, we the people united to offer any and all support possible.

That same spirit was waiting for me when I arrived here.

Whether it was somewhere to stay, a job, advice on starting out in business, credit, or materials, I was helped by an ocean of people. Some were wealthy, some were poor. Some were immigrants like me, and many were part of the Greek diaspora, while others could trace their American family ties back for generations. Some were Democrats, some Republicans or Independents. All of them had one thing in common—a willingness to extend the hand of help to someone who asked for it. The impact of this help upon my life cannot be understated. It propelled me, empowered me, and inspired me to do the same.

But while we the people are created equal, the systems and structures that exist in this world do not allow for equality of access or opportunity. It took many, many kind people to give me the opportunity to succeed, and the task continues today.

We need to cultivate that same sense of community. We need to rejuvenate our awareness of the role that small groups of people can play. We need to remind ourselves of the essential truth that lies at the heart of this country—that we, the people, hold the power to change and fix things.

## Change Starts Here

When I go to my factories, I avoid telling people what to do. Instead, I ask them, "Can you please help me?" I take time to talk to people, showing them that they're valuable and that their contribution matters.

We all need to know that our contribution matters. We all need to know that we count. Yet our government doesn't seem to agree. It wants us to be quiet, submissive, hands-off. Unless it is fighting their wars or paying their taxes, we the people seem to matter little. As far as many politicians are concerned, they're in charge. We're just there to renew their license at the polling booth every few years.

To even begin to fix this we must learn to reengage with democracy. We need to understand that democracy doesn't begin and end with our vote—though voting is absolutely essential. To fix the problems within our society, we start by becoming vocal and demanding of our political leaders the type of change that they have avoided so spectacularly for decades.

Democracy has no meaning, unless we the people take over.

Today our political leaders divide and conquer. They have given the large corporations the ability to go overseas and build products at lower cost or poorer quality than ours, resulting in the American working society paying taxes to be able to support the unemployed people.

Democracy has been hijacked by the big corporations, the media, and the lobbyists. How can it be right that a corporation can donate to the political leaders? What is happening within our democracy when a big corporation has even greater power over a politician than a citizen? How can we be so meekly obedient when all our political leaders want is for us to be obedient little consumers so they can collect more taxes? Furthermore, politicians give a lot of money out to others in order to keep them quiet and dependent on the government.

The biggest change I think we need begins with us, we the people. We must alter the way we see our purpose, refine the kind of legacy we want to leave for our descendants. It has to be more than just giving money out, sowing divisiveness, and creating chaos. We must commit to building a better foundation for the future.

So my advice to anyone who wants to make a difference is this: start a group and work together to fix things. It could be your neighbors, your wider community, your nationality, your faith group—whatever binds you together. Use it to build relationships with others and address the problems that others are ignoring.

This might sound idealistic, but I have seen it work. In both the Greek community and among my own employees, I see people who are excited about the opportunity to make a change. I see them succeed as well, and when they do they feel empowered and positive.

## Full-Citizen Leaders

So many of our leaders are stuck. They stay in post for decades, building their power base and confusing political reputation with effectiveness. They think they're serving the country, when in fact it seems a whole lot more like they're serving themselves. When we look at so many of our leaders and ask, "What have you really done to improve the country's future?" too often, it's hard to come up with an answer.

We the people must engage in politics, and we all need to hold the elected officials responsible. How? We need to talk with them when they are asking for our vote, to find out where they stand on the issues that matter most to us for our country. We need to vet them fully, to do our due diligence in order to know whether they really do have the credentials, the experience, and the character to take on the role of representing us. It's no little matter, and our votes are precious. We should exercise the same, and even greater, caution and diligence when choosing a politician to support as we do when we're looking for a builder, a babysitter, a teacher, or a surgeon.

At the end of the day, we the people are the ones holding the wheel in a democracy. Democracy is we the people, and we have lost our grip. We have given the political leaders full power of managing of our future. Unfortunately, many of them simply don't have the skills or experience required for the task. Take transportation, for example. We currently have a secretary whose only previous experience in office was acting as mayor of a city of a population of around one hundred thousand. Surely, we can demand better than that.

I don't just want to point out what's wrong. I want to suggest how—as we the people—things can be fixed. So here are seven areas where I believe we could—and should—take action.

## 1. Transform Education and Full Citizenship

For so many people, education is the first priority. If we are to level the playing field, we must address the consequences of how costly education is and how out of reach it is for those living in poverty. I was fortunate to have parents who valued schooling, and I was able to access good education in Athens. Others need help.

Finding equality in education is vital. It allows us to debate what's good for our future generations, what's good for the citizens of our country, the citizens of our continent, the citizens of our planet.

I believe that our country could pay part of our students' higher education costs, but in return the students must serve their country. By doing so, they will become full citizens.

Yes, that's right.

I believe that if we want leaders who are going to truly serve the country, we should all be prepared to do likewise. If we want better leaders, we need to be better citizens.

This will give future generations a deeper understanding

of what I call full-citizen dynamics—a system where all young people serve the country when they either finish high school or finish undergraduate school. They could serve local community programs, assist with infrastructure projects, serve the logistics of our country, be used to tackle some of the pressing social issues of the day. They could teach new immigrants English so that they, too, can become more productive members of both the community and the economy, and together we will all succeed. Can you imagine how much all that labor would benefit our country? It will free millions of workers to build American products that we desperately need. It's not exactly radical—the Post-9/11 GI Bill became effective on August 1, 2009, and has the most comprehensive education benefits package since the original GI Bill was signed into law in 1944. It pays all public school in-state tuition and fees. Why not extend it?

## 2. Get a New Vision for Trade and Immigration

Everybody's talking about immigration, but all our elected officials seem to be unable to debate and come up with a comprehensive immigration system. Over too many decades, no party has done anything constructive.

Trade is no better. Our leaders, starting at the end of twentieth century, have created a monstrosity out of trade agreements, and we the people have let them. We outsource our manufacturing to people in poor countries, who produce products that we would be able to produce ourselves. As a result, our workers are unemployed, and the government uses tax dollars to pay their compensation. We feel that we have been winning when we get cheap electronics, house appliances, and inexpensive clothing, but overseas workers are being abused and suffering, and our own labor market has become a consumer to the lower-cost countries, and people have lost their jobs. The only winners are the big corporations and the governments, especially our geopolitical adversaries, China in particular.

The imports we want should be products that other countries can make better than us, not cheaper than us. And there should be a flow of exports to equally match the imports. Instead, we have exploited countries' labor forces to get short-term gains. We have taken the easy path and sacrificed our economic future. We looked to the Far East but failed to develop trade in South America, and all because large corporations had our politicians in their pockets. The levels of migration from South America are a clear sign of our failure to build the region and unlock its potential. It could be a continent that produces and competes with the rest of the world, and if that were so, their citizens would be far more likely to experience peace and prosperity and would choose to remain at home, in the countries they love, rather than trying to migrate to the United States.

The legacy we leave behind is that we have created a very fragile and a very divided future for the planet. Rather than having some equality, we have created a very serious worldwide geopolitical strategy and dependency that the West is going to be suffering because of for a long time.

George E. Danis

Instead of pursuing equality, we have closed our eyes to what is happening. In many ways we are presiding over a system of another type of slavery—though we don't call them slaves. We accept the mistreatment of workers if it leaves more money in our pockets or means better returns on our investments. Our political leaders have been preaching human rights, but, unfortunately, they have been practicing hypocrisy.

We have lost the war. We depend on so many other countries in so many sectors of our economy. It is time for our leaders to bring jobs back, to reject one-way trade deals, and to work to create a world where our neighbors to the south can benefit from our growth and keep their citizens at home.

## 3. Level the Tax

Our tax system is totally inappropriate. It allows people to hoard millions and billions of dollars in trusts and pay no taxes, then give money to any entity that they choose to boost their ego. They think that they have done something great, something that will benefit the country and the planet, but for many it is just a thinly veiled tax break—a possible reaction to the sense that the political leaders have mismanaged their tax dollars.

We need a tax system that levels the playing field, one that ensures that everyone pays a fair amount of tax. We need a system that does not penalize the low- and mid-wage earners. Our educational institutions, hospitals, and many other institutions get all their gifts tax free while millionaires and billionaires protect their money in foundations, but every citizen with low to mid wages who is trying to save money for their children's education has to pay taxes first. How is that fair? How is that a reflection of "all men are created equal"?

The publicly traded companies hoard their profits by accumulating reserves and refuse to pay appropriate dividends to their shareholders. How is that fair?

The capital gains tax must be overhauled. We need to look at it carefully, for if you buy a stock today and you sell it tomorrow, you pay the same rate of tax as you would if you had held on to it for five years. What is the incentive for people to invest for the long term?

We need to make taxes more equitable across all taxpayers, rather than penalize the citizens who don't have the ability to hoard and use the system that protects only the large corporations or millionaires and billionaires. We need to change all this and learn how to use our tax system in a way that builds a stronger future economy for all of our citizens.

## 4. Act on Climate

Right now we have a big job to do regarding the climate issue. Whether or not we believe that all the weather changes are human related, logic and common sense tell us that if we continue to burn fossil fuel continuously, our planet is going to suffer.

When we look at the Ukraine war, we can see there are some familiar problems at work. The Europeans' consumption of energy from Russia left them exposed after the invasion, and I believe it should serve as a warning to us all. As the climate continues to be unpredictable, we place ourselves at risk if we do not transition to reliable, sustainable, efficient fuels.

I believe we need our leaders to act boldly and with a long-term plan of over twenty-five years with the private sector and the citizens of the planet. They must stop pursuing vanity projects that add little long-term value to the green economy—like so many wind farms that are financial black holes. Instead, we need to be ruthless about adopting the technologies that are going to wean us off fossil fuels. Our leaders must incentivize and mandate the private sector and their leaders to innovate, encouraging research and development through tax policies. Any tax deferrals granted must be linked to positive results, not simply handed out before research has begun. This way we can bring jobs back home.

## 5. Rip Up Foreign Policy

Sadly, we have not been very good at foreign policy. Back in the 1980s, when Russia invaded Afghanistan, we supported Bin Laden to extricate Russia from Afghanistan but, in the process, created a monster, and he came after us on 9/11.

Decades later we are still making mistakes invading and destroying Afghanistan and, twenty years later, withdrawing troops in such a chaotic way that we handed our enemy a great victory in their abuse of the Afghan people.

We have allowed our political leaders to get away with substandard performance, to be shortsighted and looking only for today. Whether sending troops to Afghanistan, Iraq, Vietnam, or Korea before that, we built governments and divided Korea (creating a monster in North Korea by keeping them divided and preventing the Korean reunification), and today, we are now threatened with a nuclear war.

We could have had a better relationship with Putin when he first came to power, but the leaders of NATO inducted neighbors of Russia into NATO, isolating Putin out of Europe. If they had truly wanted to expand democracy, they would have talked, but instead they acted to protect their own economic interests by selling military equipment to new NATO members. In the 1960s the Soviets tried to play the same expansion game, placing missiles in Cuba. Fortunately, the U.S. government had appropriate leaders and was able to negotiate and persuade Nikita Khrushchev to remove the missiles from Cuba and avoid a nuclear war.

We create problems for generations down the line, spending billions and billions of dollars in armaments to fight a war. It's not just the United States, for in my homeland they are spending more on armaments than they're spending on their people. We will spend and fight and die for overseas war games, but we have really lost our will to improve the quality of people's lives, in every sector.

Our wars have become intrinsically linked with our military industrial complex. As was said by President Eisenhower, they're good for business. As for the people doing the fighting and the dying, the rates of suicide among veterans are a clear indication of how little our leaders really do value our troops.

We must demand change. If we had a system of national service, our young people would get involved in our foreign policy.

We need transparency about the financial links between our politicians and the big corporations that profit from war. We need clarity about the influence of lobbyists over lawmakers. And when there are wars to be fought, we the people—the ones who do the fighting and the dying—need to be far more vocal about how our military will be used. Only then can we loosen the grip that the big corporations whose sole motive is making profit have on our leaders.

## 6. Fix Health Care

Our health-care system is inadequate, totally overwhelmed, and clogged. There are not enough doctors, especially for new patients, and many have wait lists a year long. Political leaders keep telling us how they're going to fix the system and how the health-care bill passed by the Obama administration was to going to address the issues. Nothing was fixed. It was just rhetoric.

I pay health insurance for my people from day one, and I believe that we should mandate that if you employ people, then you must pay for their health care, period. If you can't afford it, then the government could/should subsidize, as they do now with the present system.

Our schools are training too few doctors, and too many of those they do train are foreign students, who leave the country after they graduate. The government should mandate that the medical schools accept a minimum of 20 percent to 25 percent of applicants and not the 4 percent to 5 percent that they do now. We the people need to really demand that this be fixed quickly. We need to demand that our politicians use the power they have to change the medical schools and large corporations that have been gobbling up so many of the smaller hospitals. We the people need to remind our leaders that it is us they serve, not the corporations. Our political leaders have allowed the hospitals to become monopolies. Twenty to thirty years back, every city and town had a community hospital; now large groups have purchased all the small hospitals around and have absolute power. They have privatized the most essential service, turning health care into profit-hungry, big-hospital institutions.

## 7. Be Generous

When I arrived in the United States, I assumed that life would be the same here as it was back in Greece. In many ways it was, and the Greek community in particular extended the same warmth, welcome, and support that I was accustomed to back home. But there were so many times when I found life difficult. The language was a barrier for me, as it continues to be today for so many immigrants. When I became a business owner, I provided an opportunity to learn English to my employees by sending them to the Berlitz School of Languages, and I'm still committed to providing English language training for any people I employ who need it.

I also struggled to comprehend the systems and

expectations around how people work. I was shocked to find that in America there was nothing like the same sense of unity I experienced at home.

When I was working for companies like Honeywell and was given people to manage, I was demanding of my team. But I was also protective of them. I understood that success was something we all were invested in. Many of my first bosses were surprised by the amount of hard work and commitment I was able to motivate and produce from the people that I managed.

They were also surprised when I lobbied for the monthly bonus that was paid to the managers to be paid to all the staff.

On the first day that I started my own business, I bought lunch from Kentucky Fried Chicken for everyone, sat down with them, and we ate together.

I still do that today, bringing in lunch so that we can all eat together whenever I visit any of my plants. There's nothing better than getting together, eating, and talking like this. We exchange ideas and thoughts, all sitting around the same table.

I don't just stop at lunch. Any profit I make I am careful to share with the team. I've been doing it all my working life—investing in people, living Greek—and I know that I would be nowhere if I didn't have the people working with me.

People often make a fundamental mistake when it comes to building a business. They think that generosity runs counter to profitability. That could not be more wrong. Generosity and profitability are perfectly compatible. Rewarding your people well is one of the best strategies for the performance, commitment, and retention of your employees. When employees see that their hard work is properly rewarded, they become better motivated, more rounded, more satisfied.

Success should be shared, not put out of reach of the workers. Some people will call this socialism, but I call it taking care of your people. I am not against profit. I like profit. I like capitalism and have seen it transform many, many lives, including my own. But it works well only if the playing field is level.

Thank you very much for reading my recommendations. And now you can read the story of my journey.

George E. Danis
Waltham, Massachusetts, May 2023

# THE ROOM AND THE CELL

IT WAS EARLY MORNING AND THE SUN was still low behind
the mountain when I took one last look around the village.
Everything was old. The ruins of the ancient castle high above
us had been there since the last days of the Roman Empire.
The fishing port in the distance must have been as old as
Aristotle and Homer—both men lived on the island. But
that morning, the oldest thing of all was not the legacy of war
or trade. It was me. I was twelve years old—officially ready
to face life like a man and accept any challenge that was laid
down before me. And that meant I was ready to leave.

Living this far up the mountainside meant there wasn't
much in the way of schooling. Just a single room in the middle of the village, where they taught the youngest among
us how to read, write, and understand why Greece was the
cradle of Western civilization. High school was in the town
of Karystos, one thousand feet down. It was controlled by
the wealthy families, and they made sure that their kids were
the only ones who attended. It wasn't open to people like
me from villages like mine.

As far as I was concerned, they could keep their school and their cozy club. I was going somewhere way better. I was leaving the island and heading to a place that was full of opportunity. I was going to study in Athens. And after that? There was only one place I wanted to go.

America.

My father loaded the mule, and my mother and I followed him down to the port. I was too excited to listen to whatever he was trying to tell me. I don't remember saying goodbye to him, either, but I do recall what it felt like to be sitting in the hot, diesel-fumed, crowded hold of an old motor schooner as it edged away from the island and set off toward the mainland. It felt like the most exciting day of my life.

My mother wasn't quite so sure. Throughout the two-hour crossing she was seasick, unable to stop herself from throwing up. I felt bad for her, really I did, but in the battle between my compassion and my excitement, there was going to be only one winner. As far as I was concerned, it was still one of the greatest days of my life, and it was only going to get better.

When we finally docked at Rafina, I happily took charge, hauling our bags out onto the dock and finding a bus that took us all the way into the center of Athens. From there it was a forty-five-minute walk dragging the bags to the bus station to take us to Peristeri, a suburb on the west of Athens. My mother was still looking pale as we found the street, and soon she became flustered as well. She couldn't remember what number house we were looking for.

It was getting dark by the time she found our destination, the home of an old friend of hers from the village. Mrs. Mpalta showed us to the separate building at the side of her home and handed my mother the key. It was small, barely ten by ten feet, but contained all the basics—a small iron bed, a single bare light bulb hanging from the ceiling, a low table just large enough to hold a kerosene stove, a single chair for a single person. The supplies we'd brought with us—eggs, potatoes, a jar of olive oil, a package of cheese, some bread, and some salt—took up most of whatever spare space there was.

I sat on the bed and watched my mother cook us some potatoes and eggs. She was trying to talk to me about the next day and what it would be like for me here in Athens, but I wasn't listening. All I could feel was raw excitement, the kind that sets your pulse racing and blocks out everything else. I was finally here, in Athens, in the very room that would be my home for the next six years as I embarked on the most exciting journey that a young man could take.

"You'll be okay," said my mother once we had eaten and I was clearing away the dishes in a bucket that I'd filled from a tap outside.

"I know," I chirped.

"You're strong."

"I know."

"And you're a smart boy. This will be good for you."

"Of course," I said, putting the dishes down. I didn't need a pep talk. I was twelve, after all. I gave her my most confident smile. "I will be fine."

We woke early the next day and made the short walk to the high school. Unlike my new room, there was no trouble finding it. All we had to do was follow the crowds. My mother enrolled me, paid for the books that I would need, and left me to face the rest of the day on my own.

It was just as I'd hoped it would be. The teachers were nice, the lessons enjoyable, and I made friends right away with the other kids in my class. Even better was the fact that not a single one of them was taller than me.

At four p.m. I said my goodbyes and headed back to my room. As I walked home, I knew that the next six years would be perfect. I was finally here, in Athens, ready to become a man. Could life be any better?

Then, just as soon as I entered the room and put down my school bag, it hit me.

She was not there.

Instead, there was a note, carefully folded and placed on the corner of the table.

*George,*
*I am sorry that I had to leave to get back home, but I know that you can take care of yourself. Make sure that you cook good food and eat well. Take care of yourself.*
*M*

I had known all along that she would stay with me only one night and then return home the next day. I had known all along that I would be living alone in this ten-by-ten room, with its single light bulb and single stove, cooking for myself, taking care of myself, protecting myself. I had known that I would not see either of my parents for several months, not until school broke up and I could return to the village for a few days. I had known all of this for weeks, ever since my parents suggested I move to Athens to continue my education. I had known it all and had agreed to it happily, but as I stood holding the note, I could feel only fear and sadness clawing at my throat.

It was all too much for me. I wanted to run out of the room, out of the city. I wanted to take the bus to Rafina and catch the first boat sailing back to the island. I wanted to be back at home, up among the mountains with the ruins and the rocks and the views that stretched miles and miles into the distance. I wanted to be back home. Not there. Not alone.

I tried to shake the feelings off by distracting myself, but I wasn't hungry, and there was nothing in the room to take my attention. Back home in the village, if I ever wanted to take my mind off something, all I ever had to do was step out of the house and run up into the mountains. But here, in the city, I knew that wasn't possible.

So I went to bed.

"God," I prayed, crying my eyes out as I gently rocked myself backward and forward, "send your angels."

For a while it worked, and I fell asleep.

But when I woke up a few hours later, I was feeling worse than ever. The sadness sat on my chest like a millstone.

I got up and felt my way to the light switch. For the longest time I just stood there, perfectly still and perfectly silent. I was thinking about going home. Could I remember the route to the bus stop? Would there even be a bus running so late? If there wasn't, how long would it take me to walk to Rafina?

I went round and round with these questions, never really approaching any kind of answer. I was locked in a vicious cycle, trapped by my own sadness and fear.

But then another question emerged.

What am I doing here?

I knew the answer to that one.

I am here so that I can go to school. I am here so that I can get an education. I am here so that I can get a job and leave.

The more I reminded myself of my goal and the steps I needed to take to reach it, the more I felt embarrassed by my sadness and nerves. I knew that I had a choice—either behave like an adult or behave like a child.

I didn't want to be a child.

So, I reached into my schoolbag, pulled out one of the textbooks, and sat on the chair. If I was going to stay awake, I decided that I might as well be studying.

---

Over the years that I spent living in that small room, I learned many of life's most important lessons. Lessons like perseverance, resourcefulness, resilience. I learned that the presence of fear is not a sign you've taken a wrong turn but an opportunity to press on and make some of your greatest leaps forward. I figured out the difference between wanting a future and doing what is required to build it yourself. I developed the habit of climbing into bed at night, thinking back over the previous day, and calling to mind every single thing for which I was grateful. I made good friends, landed good jobs, made good money, and discovered the joy of walking home at night and saving the bus fare. I fell more deeply in love with my home village while at the same time nurturing a stronger and stronger appetite to travel far from it and explore the world for myself.

In short, I did a lot of growing up in that little room.

When I left it, I really was a man.

So it was kind of shocking when, about a decade after I stood alone in the room for the first time, clutching my mother's note and choking back the tears, I found myself in another small room, feeling the same weight of sorrow and fear crush my chest.

Worst of all, I was in America, the country I had been determined to visit ever since I was a child. This was the place of my dreams, the focus of my goals, the target for which I had been aiming. I made it to America, but now that I was there, everything was going wrong. The little room I was in wasn't a rundown shack or a dead-end motel. It was a jail cell, and I was in a whole world of trouble.

I lay on the small metal bed and tried my best to take off the stress. I tried to think of everything I was grateful for—my family, my health, my community—but it didn't help. I only lay awake and listened to the sound of the other inmates shouting. There were murderers among them, and I was way out of my depth.

I forced myself to call to mind all the times that I had been out of my depth before: back in Athens when I was just a kid; on board the ship in the middle of the storm as it pitched and rolled in the middle of the English Channel, me clinging on right at the top of the antenna, aware that I was one missed foothold away from death; those six weeks in Japan when I felt like I'd landed on another planet. I told myself that I had been out of my depth so many times that I was used to it.

But no matter how hard I tried, the feelings remained. I was doomed. Everything had come crashing down, and there was no way back.

It would take a miracle to put things right.

God, send your angels.

# PART
# ONE

CHAPTER ONE

# A STORY OF LOVE, WAR, AND HOME

THE START OF MY STORY could belong to almost any place, to almost any time. It is set in a landscape that has barely changed for more than a thousand years. Pine-covered hills that sit between clear ocean waters spread out below and endless skies stretching out above. Goats threading impossible paths down treacherous descents. Olive trees that make it through brutal winters and scorching summers. So much looks just the same as it did in the days of ancient empires. For those living in the villages dotted across the land, life at the start of my story is much the same as it always has been, too. Their days follow a timeless rhythm dictated by the passing of the seasons and the needs of the community—which they must be a part of so they can survive and prosper. Most people spend their whole lives in the area, bound to each other just as tightly as they are bound to the land. If ever someone leaves, something drastic must have happened.

My father, Evangelos Georgiou Ntanis (Danis), left his

village not once, but twice. The first created a little gossip. The second sent tears flowing with fear.

My father was born into a family that lived in the tiny village of Amigdalia, a place named after the abundant almond trees that have sustained village life for generations. His parents were passionate about education, and once he finished at the local school, they took the somewhat controversial step of sending him to Athens—a half-day's journey away. There he spent several years enrolled in high school and returned home to Amigdalia with a head full of ideas about how to squeeze a few more potatoes, onions, or whatever else they could plant in order to get a few more extra drachmas from their small strips of land. These were the early years of the twentieth century, and all over Greece and beyond young men like my father were dreaming of progress and innovation. These were the days of the Wright brothers and motion pictures, of zeppelins and radio receivers, of Model Ts and Albert Einstein. It was a time when everything seemed possible but only in Europe or America. In that small village of Amigdalia, the community lived from the land and by the land.

Then came the wars.

In 1912 Greece joined with Serbia, Montenegro, and Bulgaria and rose up against the Ottoman Empire. My father was still a teenager when it began, and like so many other young men, he was called upon to fight. He gave up his dreams of progress, said goodbye to his family and the people of Amigdalia, and went to war to defend and serve his country, like all of us must do if we are going to consider ourselves true citizens and not just guests.

The Turks were pushed back and the war won, yet my father was wounded and then captured, taken thousands of miles away to France, and pressed to fight in the First World War. But eventually, seven years after he left, he returned home to his family and to his village. He slipped back into the simple, timeless life of a farmer. It was time to settle down.

Progress was slow to arrive in villages like Amigdalia, but just as in small communities the world over, gossip traveled fast. When he heard people talking repeatedly about a woman in the next village, my father paid attention.

Her name was Styliani, and she was of a similar age, from a similar village, Komito, just a little further back and closer to the town of Karystos but up in the hills. Like my father, she spent several years away from Greece. And just like my father, her young life had already been touched by suffering.

Like almost every other woman at the time, she had no formal education. Yet she was intelligent and curious and as a child had closely observed her brothers while they were completing their homework. She learned to read and write that way and developed a lifelong passion for education.

As a teenager, Styliani was sent by her father to work as a housekeeper for a wealthy family in Athens. But later, when the family moved to Cairo for the husband's work, they invited her to join them. For a young woman with as much curiosity as my mother, it was a wonderful opportunity. Cairo was a world away from the little village where she grew up, and she embraced the adventure as a sunflower yearns for the sun. Yet, after a year and a half, her employer died, and she had to write to her father, asking him to send her a return ticket back home. Back to the village, back to her old life. She soon married a local farmer and bore him two sons—Evangelos and Polychronis. The excitement and adventure of Cairo were over, and the local school that her sons attended was a single room with more than sixty children crammed inside. To make matters worse, the schoolmaster was an alcoholic, who often abandoned his lessons in favor of drinking with his friends.

She was not happy about it and persuaded her husband to buy a house in a larger village called Mili, where the boys would have access to better schools and be closer to Karystos and Athens to continue their education. But before they could move to Mili, her husband contracted tuberculosis and died.

Stuck in the old village, trapped by grief, and worried about her sons' futures, Styliani decided to act and drafted a letter to the department of education complaining about the schoolmaster. Other mothers were equally unhappy, but she knew that few of them would be prepared to add their names to her letter. So, working with her sons and father-in-law, she simply forged the signatures of her neighbors at the end of her letter.

It worked. The education department sent an inspector, who found the schoolmaster drunk and incompetent. The schoolmaster was sacked, nobody discovered the forgeries, and a replacement teacher was sent to the village. Soon after she arrived and discovered how poorly the students had been taught, she started recruiting people in the local community and surrounding villages who might be able to help. Styliani was at the top of this new teacher's list. So, too, was my father, whose two nephews were also at the school.

Back then, a widow with two children had little chance of remarrying, especially a woman as headstrong as Styliani. But there were so many things about her that my father was drawn to: her passion for education, her love of family, her desire to not turn her back on an imperfect situation but stay and work hard to improve it. These are timeless qualities that have served people well for millennia. If we want a guide for how to live well today, these three will take us far.

Within six months they were married. Later the family of four moved to Mili, but before the move they sold all the land they had in the village and purchased more land in Mili. They also bought a water mill, where Mili's residents would bring the wheat they'd grown to be made into flour so they could make bread. It was a good move, as it provided the family with income.

They had two children together—me first, then my brother, Alexandros. After so much turmoil and sorrow, life was finally settling. The future was bright and clear. At least, that's how it was for a while: bright and clear, until war broke out.

I was only three when the German occupation of Greece began. Many of my earliest memories are hazy, but fear has a way of burning through the fog. I can clearly remember the nights when it was so warm that we slept outside, only to be woken up by the thunderclap of bullets and the flame of muzzle flash in the mountains above Mili as they fought the Greek resistance fighters. I remember the tension in my parents' voices whenever German soldiers were spotted in the distance approaching the village. They would tell us to gather all the wheat we had stored at home and help load it into the wooden boxes they had buried in the ground. Once it was safe, we had to round up the chickens and hide them as well.

"Now go!" my father would yell as soon as we were done. My two older brothers would lead Alexandros and me away from the village, our bare feet scrambling over the rocks, lungs screaming with pain as we ran up into the hills to hide ourselves.

In the years following the war, the true extent of German atrocities would come to light—the looting, the massacres, the annihilation of towns and villages. But even then, in the quiet corner of the island of Evia, we knew that our occupiers could do and take whatever they wanted. We were defenseless against the Germans. The best we could hope for was to be ignored.

As well as bombs and bullets and burning buildings, one of Germany's greatest weapons against us was hunger. In Athens alone, tens of thousands of people died from starvation. Even in Mili our hunger drove some of us to desperate measures.

I must have been six years old on the day that I decided to walk down the hill with a friend and go swimming in the sea. My mother reminded me where the German machine gun posts had been set up and told me to avoid the soldiers, just as every parent always did in those days. I had no intention of going anywhere near them, and my friend and I planned a route that would keep us well clear of any trouble. As we entered the town down a quiet backstreet, we saw something unexpected: a German soldier driving alone in a pick-up truck. In the back were at least fifty loaves of bread. It was a captivating sight, and for the longest time the two of us were turned to stone, staring at the truck as it idled slowly along the road ahead of us.

I was often hungry in those days, but thanks to the fact that our house had the flour mill and my parents took 10 percent of whatever they milled for local farmers, we always had wheat at home. For my friend, however, the pain of hunger was far sharper, and seeing all that bread in the truck ahead was too much. Without warning he sprinted up to the truck, grabbed a single loaf, and turned to flee.

The German soldier must have seen him, for the truck slammed to a halt and the soldier burst out of the cab. My friend was quick, but the soldier was quicker. Within seconds the man grabbed hold of my friend, placed his hands on either end of his forearm, and brought his knee up sharply in one single, violent motion. The sound of my friend's arm snapping like a piece of dry firewood filled the street.

The German returned to the truck and drove away, leaving my friend screaming in agony for a while before he passed out. Seeing him crumpled on the ground, my stomach sick with fear, I ran screaming for help.

My friend's arm was treated, but the fear left its mark upon both of us.

When the war was finally over and my country was free again, many hoped that life would return to the tranquil state it had been in for generations. But that was not to be. Throughout much of the occupation, Greece had also been fighting a civil war. With the Germans now gone, the fight for the future of Greece became even more intense. My eldest brother, Evangelos, was drafted to fight against the rebels, though my parents largely stayed clear of the politics. Instead, they poured themselves into the family, especially us two younger boys. Drawing from the wisdom that had been handed down from generation to generation, they set about teaching us one of the most important lessons of all: harmony.

Despite my father's training in commerce, the fact that he owned a flour mill, and my parents' commitment to education, my parents still saw themselves as farmers. They were not looking to escape from Mili or pursue a middle-class life in Athens. They were happy where they lived, happy to be connected to the physical world around them. Like their ancestors before them, they both depended on the land for their survival. For both my parents, one of the secrets to a good life was learning to live in step with nature.

From a young age my brothers and I were taught how to farm. We learned how to plant, tend, and harvest crops of corn, wheat, onions, potatoes, tomatoes, lemons, and more. We took care of the animals daily—milking the sheep and the goats and feeding the chickens, the pair of horses, and the mule. My mother made cheese with the milk and clothes and blankets from the wool. When we needed meat, my father would slaughter a chicken, sheep, or goat, keeping the skins to serve as containers for anything from olive oil to wine. People paid to use the mill by giving us 10 percent of their flour, so if we ever needed money for shoes or something else that we could not make or barter, my father would sell one of the sheep or the lambs or some of the olive oil that we had pressed from the olive trees we owned. We were a lot closer to poverty than wealth, but life felt rich and full. Even at a young age I could see how things were connected: when each of us carried out the work that we had been given—and if we had some good fortune courtesy of Mother Nature—we had enough food to eat and clothes to wear. We were dependent on each other and on the natural world in which we lived.

Mili sits in the foothills of Mount Ohi and directly beneath the St. Elias mountainside. All around there are steep hills and an almost total absence of level ground. One way or another, any errand I was given—taking the goats to graze farther up the mountain or running down to Karystos for supplies—would either begin or end with a bone-jarring descent and a leg-cramping ascent. The terrain challenged me constantly, strengthening my heart, lungs, and legs with the steep incline, toughening the soles of my feet as I ran barefoot across goat tracks littered with thorns and sharp rocks. In those days, when our only transport was our feet, we were all shaped by Mili, literally.

It wasn't just nature that we lived in harmony with. As a community we were deeply connected to each other. Mili was home to a couple hundred people, and even today it remains the kind of place where everybody knows not just each other's names but their failings, their faults, their secrets, and their strengths. To live in a village like Mili is to experience a way of community life that was common to everyone on the planet until the first cities were cut from the earth. At harvest time the villagers would gather with their immediate neighbors, unite as a single labor force, and work together to gather whichever crops were ready. The owner of the land would provide wine and homemade pasta for lunch, and after a hard day's work, we would spend hours feasting and talking together. When people would get tired beneath the fierce sun, someone would call out, "Together we can win!" It is difficult not to maintain good relationships with your neighbors when you rely upon each other so much.

Church played a significant part in our lives as well. We attended every Sunday, accompanied by everyone else in the village. On festival days when we were given communion, all of us children would spend the hour before the service began visiting our neighbors and asking them a simple question.

"Please, would you forgive me for anything I have done which has offended you?"

Most of the time my neighbors would have cause to be angry with me. I often helped myself to whatever fruit I wanted from whatever land I happened to be in, and most of my friends loved to play tricks on people, like the time we threw firecrackers near a woman who was carrying a basket filled with grapes. The noise gave her such a fright that she dropped the whole basket and watched the grapes scatter halfway down the track to Karystos. But in spite of my behavior, whenever I asked for forgiveness, nobody held anything against me. It was the same for my friends too: we would knock on the doors of the people on whom we had played tricks and be shown nothing but love and acceptance in return.

Only years later—decades even—would I come to understand quite how unusual this all was and how deeply it impacted my life. It taught me the importance of swiftly acknowledging when you have made a mistake and hurt someone and of offering forgiveness when the wounds are yours. But there is more to it than that. As I have grown older, I have come to understand how powerful it is to be loved and accepted not just by your family but by your community as well. When we know that we truly belong, we are able to be who we were made to be.

Church was central to village life, and not just for Sunday services, life events, or feast days. It was our moral compass, our North Star. It taught us how to live well with each other—confessing, forgiving, supporting as if we were one large family of flesh and blood. We took that scripture about loving your neighbor as you would yourself seriously.

In the previous decades before my birth, the community had been tested. Both my parents and my grandparents knew war as well as the sudden trauma of economic collapse. If they hadn't known how to support each other through desperate times, I doubt whether as many of them would have made it through.

Throughout my early childhood I was constantly taught about the importance of living in harmony with the natural world and the community around me. Most of the time I was a willing student, eager to follow the guidance that was given me. There were times, however, when I needed a firmer hand.

I was out playing with my friends one day when my mother called to me and asked me to come back to the house to collect a large jar and then go collect some water from the spring a little way up the hill. It must have been during the occupation, for I remember feeling particularly glad that there were no German soldiers in the area that day. So, while I told my mother that I would do it right away, I didn't. I was having too much fun playing with my friends.

As soon as I saw my mother marching toward me, I knew that I had messed up. She glanced at the empty jar lying on the ground nearby and gave me one of those looks that froze my feet to the spot. "Why haven't you brought the water back?"

I shrugged. "I forgot."

There was a brief but heavy silence. "Okay," she said when she was done thinking. "Let's do it now."

I picked up the jar and struggled to keep up with her as she marched on toward the spring. When we were there, she watched as I filled it, then had me pick it up and follow her back home. All the time there was silence between us, but

I didn't mind. The jug was heavy even without the water, so when it was full it was a real struggle for a skinny little kid like me.

As soon as we stood in the yard at home, she took the jug from my hands. She tipped it up and emptied the water all over the stones.

"Okay, George," she said, handing me the now-empty jug. "Now you can go back and fill it again."

I was both annoyed and confused, but I knew better than to say anything rude to her. Instead, I told her I would, picked up the jug again, and headed straight back toward the stream.

"Don't forget to come back this time, George!"

I held my tongue all the way to the spring and all the way back home. I was quiet and more than a little moody as I handed over the water, but again I knew better than to say anything. We were a peaceful and harmonious family, but we children never disrespected our parents.

"Thank you, George," she said when I was finished. "Now you can go back and play with your friends."

I paused. She must have sensed my unspoken question as the next moment my mother placed a hand on my shoulder and looked deep into my eyes.

"If someone tells you to do something, you might forget. When you see it being done, you remember it. But it is only when you do it yourself that you finally understand. It's true for all things in life."

It did not take too many episodes like the time with the jug for me to learn what was expected of me. Yet it would be years before I could truly appreciate the depth of the wisdom and the value of the lessons that I was taught during these early years.

My mother's way of teaching me became a method I use and encourage in everyone who works for me. If we expect people to do a good job, we must explain what we want, give opportunity to practice, ask questions, and then step out the way and let them get on with it. We need to empower employees to taste success for themselves, not treat them like servants. We must treat people as equals, no matter their wage or their job title. We must recognize that businesses only truly succeed when everyone feels as though they are invested in winning.

From my earliest days as a business owner, I also made it a priority to regularly buy lunch for my workers and sit and eat with them, sharing my vision for the company and listening to their feedback. We would host barbecues and cookouts and encourage everyone to bring their family along, and I still continue those traditions today as I visit different plants. Sometimes as we're sitting around a break room eating pizza and chicken, I find myself telling people about what it was like to work side by side with your neighbors to harvest sackfuls of olives under a cloudless Mediterranean sky. It sounds exotic, but I tell them there's very little difference, really. The same essential truth runs through our veins: "Together we can win."

When I look out at the world today, it strikes me that despite all that has changed in the way we live and work, the ancient wisdom that my parents and their ancestors followed is just as relevant. We were not created to live in isolation. We are not made to exist alone. We are better when we are connected, not just to each other but to the planet that sustains us.

This doesn't just apply to us as members of small communities. It relates to us as citizens as well. We live in a democracy, and our responsibilities don't just stop when we leave the voting booth. In fact, that's really when our duties start. We should be communicating with our elected officials on all the issues that aren't working for our county's future. We should be demanding that the people we voted for are listening to us and correcting the policies that are flawed. How else can we obtain sustainability for our future?

## CHAPTER TWO
# AN ENGINEER'S MIND

"You have nails on your seat, George! Why can't you sit still?"

This was a constant cry from my mother. I was always moving, never sitting still. But it wasn't just that my body that was full of energy; my mind was always racing, always active. I was curious—and not just the kind of curiosity that leads a child to constantly ask questions or to wonder out loud why the clouds are white or the grass is green. My curiosity was on a whole other level. As I looked at the world around me—especially the tools and machines that we relied upon for our livelihood—my mind was full of *what ifs* and *I wonder what will happen when*. I had little desire to share these thoughts with my parents, for instinct led me to believe that talking about my curiosity was likely to get it shut down. So I kept my thoughts to myself and learned to operate under the radar as I set about my tasks. The results were mixed.

Like every other family living in Mili, we were poorer than those living at the bottom of the hill in the town of Karystos. There were only two miles between us, but the differences were vast. Karystos was built at the end of the nineteenth century, at a time when Greece was full of optimism about the future—a future in which Karystos might one day grow to rival the great city of Athens. Right from the start it was built with progress in mind, with the streets laid out in a grid formation and the port deep enough for the trade schooners to sail direct to Athens, laden with lemons, olives, potatoes, onions, grapevines, oregano, freshly picked bunches of mountain tea, and other wonderful produce grown in villages like Mili and beyond. When I was a child, Karystos was home to many wealthy merchants. Their lives were full of luxuries that nobody in the village could hope to afford.

Karystos was the future, and to my eyes, it seemed that kids in Karystos had everything they could ever want. Whenever I was in the town, either collecting something for my parents or going through it to swim in the ocean, I made a careful study of the latest toy that I saw my privileged neighbors enjoying. Inevitably, my envy collided with my curiosity, and I tried to figure out a way to replicate their toys without spending any money.

It started with hoops. I was six or seven when the streets of Karystos were full of children playing with two-foot-high metal hoops, which they rolled along the ground using a wooden stick. It required a little skill and looked like a lot of fun. From my research gazing in shop windows, I also knew that a hoop-and-stick set was expensive. But I was not deterred and set my mind to finding an alternative.

I found the solution hanging on the wall in the tiny

George E. Danis

storeroom at home, where my father kept some of his tools, including the spare parts for the oak barrels that he used to store excess wine in the event of a particularly good harvest. The metal hoops that gave the barrels their structure were the perfect size—even having the advantage of being a little wider than the ones I'd seen in the town, which I was convinced would make them easier to keep upright. Even better was the fact that there was also some heavy-duty wire in the storeroom, which I decided to use instead of a stick. I spent ages carefully bending one end of the wire into a kind of hook that would fit perfectly around the hoop, making it far easier to control. I took my new toy outside, ran through a brief period of testing and adjustment, then demonstrated it to my friends in the village—all the time being careful to avoid any adults seeing us. My friends all agreed that it was way better than what the rich kids down in Karystos were buying.

The only problem was durability. After an hour or more of heavy play along the rocky streets of Mili, the hoop was too bent out of shape to roll, so I returned it to the storeroom and took a replacement from the wall. I took another when that second hoop was used up and another after that. Before long all the spares were gone, and I faced a choice: call it quits or find another solution. I didn't quit. Instead, I turned to the few barrels that were fully made up, quickly dismantling them with a hammer and chisel.

A few months passed by the time the grapes were ready for harvest and the barrels needed to be cleaned and assembled.

By then the whole hoop-rolling trend was long gone, but I was careful to make sure that I was nowhere nearby when the dismantled barrels and out-of-shape hoops were discovered.

Even though they must have known it was me, I heard nothing about it from my parents. It was the same outcome when my peers in Karystos went wild for kites. There were days when I would descend the hill and be transfixed by the sight of a sky full of brightly colored diamonds. Buying my own kite was not an option, nor could I afford all the materials required to make one myself. So I thought hard, did my research, and found a way to construct a kite out of bamboo and newspaper. The only thing I was missing and unable to improvise was string. So I turned to the small loom that my mother used to make our woolen clothes. I carefully unpicked the thick thread that was integral to the loom and attached it to my kite. It worked perfectly, of course, and I narrowly avoided being scolded for my actions by carefully threading the string back and restoring the loom to full working order.

I was wise enough not to be a rule breaker at school, but there was as strong a need to be resourceful there as there was at home. The school was well run, but with seventy of us attending and only one school room and one teacher, we had to work together in order to learn. Older pupils helped the teacher by working alongside the younger ones, passing on what they had been taught. Not only was it far less intimidating for a young child to be taught to read, write, or work out sums by someone only a few years older than them, but it also gave the older pupils a lot of opportunity to practice and improve their communication and leadership skills.

The whole village understood that if we wanted change, we needed to deliver it for ourselves. We regularly worked together to plant trees, fix any problems, and even build a new church. We were a little isolated up there above Karystos, but that isolation made us resourceful and united. Nobody opted out when there was work to be done. Nobody was left alone.

I'm sure that whoever came up with the proverb about necessity being the mother of invention must have experienced poverty firsthand. I am deeply grateful for the fact that my family lacked the financial resources to go out and buy a lot of things, because being poorer than the families down in Karystos was the spark that ignited my curiosity and fueled my determination. If I had been simply given a hoop or handed a kite, I would have been robbed of the experience of making them for myself. I would have missed the opportunity to see where my curiosity took me, and my appetite for finding out how things work might have withered there and then. If we had been wealthy, in so many ways I would have been poorer.

It is not always comfortable to find ourselves in a position where we are unable to afford the things that we desperately want. But that need and that desire are likely far more valuable to us than whatever it is we wish we could put on our credit card. We think more deeply and engage with problems more creatively when the stakes are higher. In business as in life, we should be wary of the moment when everything is easy and comfortable.

As well as resourcefulness, my childhood bred in me a good deal of resiliency. Our house was small and my parents slept in the living room, while my three brothers and I shared the other room. Polychronis and Evangelis had the room's only bed, while Alexandros and I slept on the stone floor. In the middle of winter, the temperature would drop below thirty degrees, and Alexandros and I would lie fully clothed under blankets so heavy it was sometimes hard to move. We all had to learn how to put up with discomfort, to persist despite whatever pain we might have to endure.

This way of life didn't trouble me, and I was fit and healthy throughout nearly all of my childhood. The only times I can recall visiting the doctor were when I needed my tonsils removed at some point—a procedure carried out under local anesthetic only—and when my mother was worried about my lack of appetite and low-grade fever.

In those days the medical system was a little different, and patients would show up at the doctor's office first thing and wait to be seen in order of medical urgency. I was young then but old enough to remember the sight of the fellow patients, some of them who looked really ill.

Everyone sat up and paid attention when the doctor entered and scanned the room. I did likewise, wondering which person was sick enough to get the golden ticket and be seen first.

"You," he said, pointing at me. "I'll see you first."

There was a murmur of disagreement around the room. "You can all wait," he snapped. "The boy needs help now."

It was not long after the incident when my friend's arm was broken by the German soldier, and I had been struggling with nightmares for weeks. Today I'd say that I was anxious and perhaps a little depressed, though back then I doubt the doctor would have used the same words. But after checking me over and asking a lot of questions, he eventually told my mother that the best thing would be for me to get out of the village and spend some time somewhere else, perhaps with a relative. He asked my mother where her mother lived—she replied "Komito"—and he told her to take me there.

A couple of days later, my mother put me on the mule and led me over the mountains to her mother's village and the house her brother lived in. It took hours to reach, but I was starting to feel better even before we arrived. All that natural curiosity within me was stirring, and I was excited about the prospect of being somewhere that I had visited before but never lived.

It turned out to be even better than I expected. My uncle had three daughters, all older than me, and land that was filled with vineyards, orchards, and livestock. I was given no chores, allowed total freedom, and spent my days climbing trees, eating fruit in the orchard, and making boats in the river. I could let my imagination run free and explore whatever interested me. Though I was unaware of the significance at the time, I was discovering something that would become one of my life's guiding principles: that when we give free rein to our curiosity, life can flourish. People will be happier and healthier. They will think more deeply and work more productively at whatever they are doing.

Within a month I was fully restored and ready to return home. I was also ready to create chaos.

Not long after my return, one of my friends was given a scooter as a present. It was a beautiful thing: two wheels, a solid baseboard, and a highly varnished wooden post rising up at the front with wide, elegant handles. It was an impressive piece of craftsmanship and engineering, and I spent a long time studying it, analyzing every little detail, and committing it to memory.

Immediately, I started thinking about where I could source the materials and build my own. The wood was easy enough, but the wheels were a whole other challenge. I spent days trying to come up with a plan to get my hands on a pair, but the thinking was in vain. And then, just as I was about to give up, I had an idea.

I remembered the mill and how from time to time my father would carry out some routine maintenance on it. I'd watch him as he worked, fascinated by the sight of him and one of my stepbrothers lifting the heavy top stone off the mill and revealing the mechanism within, a mechanism which included a perfectly O-shaped metal casing with ball bearings inside that sat over the central shaft and allowed the mill to rotate. Better still, there was a spare lying around as well, and I knew they would be pretty good wheel substitutes for my scooter.

I enlisted my little brother Alexandros, swore him to secrecy, and set to work dismantling the mill. It wasn't easy, but what I lacked in muscles I made up for in determination. We soon had the mill opened up, the metal casing removed, and the stone replaced. It looked just as it had before my modification, only instead of the top stone gliding smoothly over the lower one, the whole mill refused to turn at all.

My scooter was great. Even better than I had hoped. I took it down to Karystos and sped around the tiled central plaza, drawing admiring looks from the other scooter owners. I returned home happy and exhausted.

My father was angry and exasperated. While I was down in the town, he had tried to get the mill working, diagnosed the problem, and confirmed both the cause and the culprit. Unlike the times when I dismantled the loom or repurposed the wine-barrel hoops, there was no mercy. I was punished so thoroughly that I didn't do any more dismantling without permission.

But it worked out well. He bought some replacements, and I did get to keep the ball bearings and my scooter, yet my father was unhappy. He asked me to get a job and introduced me to his friend who started a small soft drink factory, where a friend from school also worked. I was hired and started work.

The factory owner built a mezzanine where my friend and I would sleep after working late in the night. A few shifts into my job, around 2:00 a.m., my friend and I woke up to the sound of a colossal explosion across the street.

We ran outside and into total chaos. People were screaming from panic, the sidewalk was full of blood, and there were injured people walking about everywhere. A man who had just been dropped by his fiancé went to the house and threw a grenade inside—killing himself in the process.

I ran back to Mili as fast as my bare feet would carry me.

My father was so happy that I was not hurt. So happy that I didn't have to go back to the job.

# CHAPTER THREE
# ATHENS

My family home in Mili is empty now, but from the small terrace at the front, the view is just as impressive as it ever was. Look up behind you and you will see the ruins of the thousand-year-old fort that dominates the towering hills. To the front, in the distance, the Aegean Sea stretches out toward the horizon. Each day the sun arcs left to right across it, the light always falling on Mili. Closer to home, down below and crowded around the water's edge like a giant flock of pelicans at rest, are the white stone buildings of Karystos. It's busy down there, filled with weekenders from Athens and tourists from farther afield. These days shaded, peaceful villages like Mili are quiet sanctuaries. They are places to which people retreat to escape the busyness of Karystos. It was never that way when I was a child.

The people of the town had insults for villagers like me.

"Shepherd boy!"

"Go back to the goats!"

"There go the barefoot peasants!"

You'd hear the names called out if you walked by a group

of town kids. Sometimes there would be more than words, and you'd receive the occasional punch as well. It wasn't fun, but my father helped me understand.

"When the depression affected all of us," he'd say, "those people down in Karystos would come up to the village and beg us for flour. They're no better than us. Those merchants still need us today to grow the produce that they sell in Athens."

When my twelfth birthday was approaching, I knew that change was coming. My time at the one-room school in Mili would end that summer, and I faced a choice about which high school I would attend for the next six years. The nearest and most logical school for me to attend was in Karystos, but places were limited, and the competition was fierce. Rumor had it that the entrance exam was particularly difficult. Still, I was bright and hardworking, and I believed that I was as smart as any kid I knew of my age, whether they lived in Karystos, Mili, or anywhere else.

I sat for the exam and waited for the result. As the weeks passed by, I tried not to think too much about what would happen if I didn't pass and daydreamed instead about what life would be like as a student at Karystos high school. I pictured myself walking down the hill each morning, a few friends from Mili beside me, all of us excited about showing those town kids what we were capable of. I imagined myself learning new skills, exploring new ideas down in the town, and then returning home to share what I'd discovered with my parents. Their appetite for knowledge was always strong, and their encouragement of me as a student was one of the key foundations upon which my love of learning was built.

I did well on the test, better than anyone else I knew. And yet no place at the high school in Karystos was offered to me. After weeks of trying not to think about the alternative, I had to face the sudden change in my reality: I would be continuing my education in the only place where my background didn't matter. I would be heading to Athens. Alone.

School ended, and I did what I could to distract myself from thinking about Athens. I got myself a job working as a deckhand on a schooner that was sailing from the southern part of the island, delivering goods to ports way up in the north of Greece. Once or twice a week I would leave home and head to the port in the next town along from Karystos. There I would join my crew as we headed off on yet another run along the coast. It would take us a couple of days to reach as far as Thessaloniki, and I loved every aspect of the job, from the long hours spent at sea with the sails blowing full as the coast swept by to the frantic activity as we neared our destination and pulled into port. I loved the noise of the engines and the crowded docks just as much as I loved the open seas with the spray in my face and the pods of dolphins racing along with the ship.

Up until that summer, my world had been made up of Mili, Karystos, and the occasional trip over the hills to my uncle's house. I had been as far as Athens once or twice, but each of those visits felt like major expeditions. Now, everything was different. The world—or my part of it—was no longer a few villages nestled in the corner of a quiet island. In less than forty-eight hours, I could travel to the farthest part of my homeland, an area I'd barely heard of before. It was magical to be able to travel so far, so fast, and to earn a few drachmas while doing it was even more appealing. I had no idea at the time, but that summer a powerful seed was sown deep within me.

So much of that period felt mythical, yet as the hottest days started to fade and the summer winds shifted, the adventure ended. It was time to return home and pack up the food and basic supplies that my parents had gathered. Time to board a different schooner and sail across to the mainland, my mother struggling with seasickness with every rise and fall on the waves. It was time to ride the bus into the noise and chaos of Athens, to find the little room that would be my home for the next six years. Time to become a man.

That journey to Athens at the end of that summer is forever seared into my memory: my father quiet as he led us down to the harbor, my mother seasick on board the schooner, the confusion as we struggled to find the address of the woman who agreed to rent me the room. Every hour of that day I was happy, excited about the new beginning ahead of me.

And then, the next day, as I stood in the room and read my mother's note, all that happiness and optimism vanished. In an instant it was replaced by the kind of deep, lung-crushing sadness that feels as though it will never end.

I stood and stared at the letter my mother left me in that little room in Athens. I read it over and over, her words echoing hollow inside me. I was unable to stop crying.

In that moment, in that room, I felt more like a child than I had ever felt before. It was as if all the worst feelings I'd ever had were returning—the shock of seeing that German soldier snap my friend's arm, the sense of dread as I realized my curiosity had landed me in trouble yet again, the humiliation as a bunch of boys in Karystos yelled out their taunts—only now the feelings were combined and intensified.

Reaching for my textbook was the only thing I could think of that would distract me that evening. It worked, though I didn't sleep much that night. The next morning, I woke up, and a little of that same dread and sorrow was weighing me down. I wondered about skipping school and going to sit in a park instead, but having decided that I was there to learn, I showed up for my lessons on time.

This was the pattern I followed for the first few days and weeks of my new life alone. I tried my best to block out the sadness and focus on my studies, and most of the time I was successful. When I was at school I felt fine, but the long hours I spent alone in my room became a daily battle. It didn't take long for me to start looking around for something else besides my studies to distract me.

I found just the distraction I needed when I stepped inside a local pool hall. I'd never seen the game played before, let alone picked up a cue or tried to apply the laws of geometry at the table. But as I stepped in from the street, listened to the clacking of the balls and the low buzz of friendly conversation, and saw the ranks of green-topped tables bathed in sacred light like works of art, I was hooked.

The first week or two I was happy just to watch, but eventually I wanted to play. Each game cost a few drachma—hard-earned money that I had been given by my parents with a solemn instruction to spend it only on the absolute essentials—but I soon forgot about being wise with my money or doing what my parents told me. Playing pool gave me the excitement and the distraction that I craved. When I was hunched over the table, thinking about force and angles and the laws of physics, everything else—the room, the distance between Athens and home, the ache of remembering what it felt like to be held by my mother—all faded just a little further back into my mind.

Pool offered me something else as well: community. When I was there in the hall with the happy murmur of conversation all around, I felt comfortable again, as if I were with family.

I'd been going to the pool hall every day after school—as well as most of the weekends—for about two weeks, when everything changed. I was midway through a game with one of the regulars and was finally looking like I was about to win a game, when I heard a familiar voice shout my name.

I spun round and saw my brother Polychronis storming across the pool hall toward me. I froze, cue in hand, terrified. I had always respected and feared my elder brothers as much as I feared my parents. Within seconds he was standing right in front of me, throwing away the cue with one hand and grabbing me by the ear with the other. A few seconds later I was dragged out onto the street, where Polychronis was yelling at me about how foolish I was to waste the opportunity our parents had given me.

Besides being eleven years older than me, Polychronis was also an officer of the Athens police force. He was used to talking to people who had made bad choices and knew just what to say to make me wake up and change my mind.

"If I catch you again somewhere like this, I'm gonna kill you. You understand?"

I nodded, my legs suddenly losing nearly all their strength. I wasn't sure that he'd actually kill me, but I was in no doubt at all about how miserable he'd make my life if I carried on wasting my time and our parents' money like this.

From then on, I was instructed by Polychronis to stop looking for distractions. Instead, I would walk over to his workplace to find him and spent my time more wisely. When I didn't have schoolwork to do, I would make the ninety-minute walk across the city to Polychronis's office. I'd eat in his cafeteria, sit quietly at his desk, and feel the warmth of being close to my brother once again. And, if Polychronis was busy, I'd walk another thirty minutes and visit one of my uncles in whatever restaurant he was eating. Again, I would fill myself up with good food and good loving company. However, I was not feeling free and as independent as I wanted; I thought Polychronis had set the rules that I must obey, otherwise I would be punished by my older brother.

But it all helped, and when Christmas came around, I made my first return trip to Mili to see my parents. I was happy to be able to spend time with my family, friends, and neighbors, and it was always fun to be around the family during Christmas and the New Year. I still miss it today.

I returned to Athens and started the new year with a fresh sense of excitement. I was ready to be challenged with my schoolwork and cared for by my brother. Even though I had to walk a round trip of three hours to see him, it was well worth it because his advice and support were things I could rely on. My foundations were firm, my roots solid. It was time to get a job.

Polychronis introduced me to a man who owned a restaurant halfway between his office and my room, and I started as a busboy right away. For three evenings each week, I'd work from eight until midnight, clearing and laying the tables, bringing bread and water, and doing whatever else the three waiters told me to do.

Work in the restaurant was nothing like the summer I spent on the schooner. As a deckhand I was given the simplest tasks that had little to do with the running of the ship. In the restaurant, even though my tasks were as basic as fetching and carrying, it was made clear to me from the start that if I messed up, there would be serious repercussions.

"You make sure that you take care of our customers," said one of the waiters on my first night. "They are our livelihood. If you don't look after them right, we won't get tipped. And if that happens, our families won't eat. So you're responsible for my children, you understand?" The message was very stern.

He didn't have to tell me twice. Each evening I worked as hard as I'd ever worked in my life, always paying attention to both the customers and the waiters. I never let myself switch off or become distracted, and as a result I learned more about the world of work in those evenings than I learned about science or mathematics at school during the day.

I learned that there was a link between giving the customers great service, making them happy, and getting rewarded with the biggest tips.

I learned that when the waiters saw that I was reliable and hardworking, they treated me better, and they would give me a small portion of their tips.

I learned that the harder I worked, the quicker the time went.

I learned that even though my job was simple, there was something deeply satisfying about doing it well, especially when the people that I served were so happy and appreciative that they also left a few coins on the tables for the busboy.

I also learned that when I walked home at one o'clock in the morning, I needed to protect myself. I would pass by men hiding in shadows on the street, and it was wise to make sure that I didn't have all the coins that I'd earned that evening jangling together in one pocket.

And when I woke up the next morning, after only a handful of hours of sleep, I was tired but excited about the potential of everything the day held for me. Even though I had money saved and could easily have afforded a few hours of pool on the nights I wasn't working at the restaurant, I had no desire to go back to the hall. I didn't want to waste my time anymore and was afraid of the consequences from my brother as well. I wanted to be productive for as many hours of each day as I possibly could.

In short, I was discovering and nurturing one of the most valuable character traits any of us can possess: a love of any work you have to do or choose to do.

I ended my first year of high school and immediately returned to Mili, where I would have liked to spend time with my friends, but that was not a choice. Instead I resumed my previous job on the schooner. I was still just a deckhand, but something was different this time. I wanted to take on as many new responsibilities and learn as many new skills as I could.

My second year at high school started well. I was back working at the restaurant and enjoyed the new courses we were studying. The only problem was the academic workload. It was too light. I found that I could easily get all my homework done during the week, even with three shifts at the restaurant. My Saturdays and Sundays were wide open, leaving me with way too much empty time on my hands. And boredom was the last thing that I wanted to deal with.

One of my friends at school was called Aristides. He was a short, powerful guy, with wildly curly hair and a personality to match. He could talk to anyone, charming them with a smile that sparkled like the morning sun on the ocean. He had the same hunger for work that I did, but instead of working regular hours for tips in a restaurant, he told me that he had taken a different route.

"Cloth," he said. "I sell cloth."

I was confused.

"Have you seen how many people there are in the market selling cloth? Almost everybody in Athens is trying to save money wherever they can, and a lot of the women make their own clothes because they want to look good and don't want their husbands to feel that they're wasting money. But instead of setting up a stall in the market and competing with all the other traders there, I get to the customers first."

"How?"

"I knock on their doors. I take the market to them. Think about it, George. There must be almost a million women in the city, and we know where to find them. That's a lot of potential customers."

I thought about it hard.

This was different from the other jobs I'd had before. As deckhand and busboy, I was working for others. I was protected. If I was going to follow in the footsteps of Aristides, I would be on my own. If things went wrong, I'd have nobody to cover my back. It felt like a risk.

Many people don't want to take risks in life. Why? Some worry about the consequences of falling short, others about the costs of success. The reasons will vary from person to person, but the root of the matter for most people on the planet is a simple, single thing: fear of failure.

Failure is seen by so many of us as unacceptable. But ask any investor or entrepreneur to share something about the lessons they have learned along the way, and sooner or later they'll tell you the things they got wrong. They'll tell you that their hardest fails built strength and resilience. They'll talk about learning to make great decisions by seeing firsthand the consequence of bad ones. Some of them will even say that their greatest successes have been linked to some of their greatest failures.

"Feel the fear and do it anyway" goes the saying, and it's true. To experience fear is natural, but if we let it paralyze our limbs and prevent us from acting, we miss out on all the good lessons and experiences that we might otherwise go through.

That's how we learn. Standing at the doorway with an armful of cloth, summoning up the courage to knock, so many things might go wrong. And so many things *will* go wrong. But we can learn from them, and those lessons are packed full of goodness. They offer the kind of insight and experience we cannot gain anywhere else.

I decided that it was worth the risk, so I made up my mind to dive right in. Aristides let me join him, and I spent the following Saturday cold calling in a neighborhood that he said was always good for business. I was nervous ringing my first few bells and a little hesitant at first. But just like in my job as a busboy, I discovered on my first day that there was a link between the way I behaved and the way people responded. When I put aside my bashful self, unleashed a broad smile, and treated my potential customers with respect and courtesy—as well as whatever charm I could summon— they were far more interested in what I was selling. Sure, a few doors were slammed in my face, but at the end of the day, I had managed to sell most of the cloth that Aristides had given me.

I was hooked and devoted several hours each weekend to my door-to-door sales. Sometimes Aristides and I would pick a neighborhood and divide the streets between us, but other days we'd go our separate ways. After three weeks I managed to sell enough cloth to open an account with our supplier, and soon I expanded my operation so that I carried with me three different types and colors of cloth.

At the time I had no idea what foundations I was laying down for later life. All I knew was that knocking on a hundred doors in a day and having some good conversations with many nice women, with some even offering me coffee or food while I was making a handful of sales, didn't feel remotely like hard work. It felt as natural as breathing. I also learned to be very careful and avoid getting killed.

Today, however, I can clearly see how significant these early experiences were to me becoming a working adult and entrepreneur. I was learning the importance of committing myself to a task and not getting dismayed by rejection. I was learning that giving great service is not just a matter of clearing tables or bringing water but of treating someone with respect and dignity and leaving them feeling better for the time they have spent with you. Yet again, I was learning how important and helpful it is to really *need* to work. But most of all, during those days that I spent knocking on doors and preparing to greet whoever opened them with a warm smile and a ready compliment, I was learning the power of working for yourself as your own boss.

When I was selling door-to-door in Athens, I didn't care at all about cloth or making clothes, but I did care about the money I was making and the satisfaction I received from serving my customers and making people happy. As an employer, we have to help our employees find that same level of motivation and personal investment.

So many times over the years I have told people the same thing: "You might think you work for me, but you don't. I'm the one paying your wages, but really, you're working for *yourself.*"

When people see their job as being of real value to themselves, when they realize that they stand to truly share in the success of their labor, then they will be far more motivated to commit to that work.

My second year at high school passed even more quickly than the first. When it was over I again returned to Mili for the summer and worked on the schooner, racing up and down the coast and visiting different islands and ports, once again supplying people with products they needed for their everyday lives. I returned to Athens in September and this time enrolled to study technical engineering at the junior college Archimedes in Piraeus. It was an obvious course to choose and not just because of my natural curiosity for all things mechanical.

Ever since attending the school in Mili and working on the schooner that first summer, I had been thinking about what I might do with my life. It struck me that the choice

George E. Danis

was simple: either I found a job that would allow me to work somewhere far from my village, or I would end up back in Mili as a farmer. I didn't hate the idea of following in the footsteps of my father and his father before him, but I didn't love it, either. The thought of farming didn't excite me. My work as a deckhand, a busboy, and a salesman all caught my imagination. Now that I had gotten a taste for being my own boss by serving people and earning money, I longed to travel even farther from home and learn more about the planet and all of the different people of the world.

It seemed to me that being an engineer was the best way to continue pursing those exciting goals. I would find the work interesting and financially rewarding, and—perhaps most importantly of all—I would have opportunities to find work far away from Mili, far away from Athens, and maybe even far away from Greece itself.

I was young at the time but old enough to have seen a side of Greece that I wanted to leave behind. For the first twelve years of my life my homeland had been locked in a series of violent conflicts, first with Italian fascists, then with the Germans, and finally in the civil war that pitched neighbor against neighbor and family against family. I had seen enough, and I wanted to escape to a more peaceful world.

But if I left Greece, I didn't want to go just anywhere. There was somewhere specific that I had my eyes fixed upon, a destination that had captivated my imagination ever since I was sharing a room with my three brothers and sleeping on the hard stone floor at home in Mili.

Like everyone else, my memories of the early years of my childhood are blurred together. For me, the chores were never-ending, and each morning brought a repeat of the previous day's tasks. Of course there were name days celebrations and feast days and other random events that stand out in my mind, but even they have become a little hazy as the decades have passed. But there was one event that took place every year, which I have never forgotten. It was a day so special that I would spend weeks anticipating its arrival and just as long savoring it once it had passed. It was the day that my mother's brother, who lived in the United States, sent us gifts.

Most times the presents arrived in a suitcase. A reverent silence would fall over us all as the case sat in the living room, waiting until everyone was back home in the evening. Only then would we be allowed to gather round and watch while one of my parents carefully unlocked and undid the buckles, released the catches, and lifted the lid, all the time working with the calm precision of a surgeon.

My three brothers and I would strain to see what was inside, and we were never disappointed. Our uncle always sent a lot of clothes, and one time there was a basketball that needed to be inflated before Alexandros and I ran with it, triumphant, out of the house and into the village to parade it before our neighbors. Another time the gift was so large it wouldn't even fit in the case: it was a real live mule, shipped all the way from Philadelphia.

I'd never met my uncle, but his gifts made a significant

impression on me. Later, I would come to understand and appreciate the importance of generosity, and I have been following that tradition of being generous whenever I can show it to others. When I was a child, however, I was simply impressed that anyone could not just afford but have access to so many wonderful items. Those suitcases shaped my fourteen-year-old aspirations. They created in me a sense that the United State was the place I needed to go. I became convinced that there, in the land where my uncle was thriving, I would be able to test myself. It was there that I would surely be able to succeed.

# CHAPTER FOUR
# THE *ATLANTIC SEA*

ONCE I HAD DECIDED THAT AMERICA was my destination of choice, I needed to figure out a way to get there. That bit was easy. I'd met a lot of merchant marines during my summers on the schooner, and I heard a lot of them talking about the places they'd been. Japan was mentioned a lot, as were Poland, Germany, and the United States. I didn't care much for those first three, but as long as I ended up somewhere in America, I'd be happy.

At fifteen I was still too young to land a job on board one of the giant freighters that made these epic ocean voyages. I needed more time and more skills, so once I finished my three years at the high school, I enrolled in a three-year marine engineering course at the junior college Archimedes in Piraeus, the central hub of the entire Greek shipping industry.

I carried on working the same jobs as before but kept an eye out for opportunities to land a position on a crew. The second year passed by without any hope of a job appearing, but I didn't worry too much. I told myself that the next year—when I would turn seventeen and complete my mechanical engineering training—would be when I found a job. My college mates felt the same way. We were all looking for work throughout the year, and despite being right there in Piraeus, success was rare.

I finished the year and intensified my search. I went to every shipping company's office that I could find, visiting each of them weekly. Years of selling cloth to the housewives of Athens taught me to be resilient in the face of rejection, but as the weeks passed by and I failed to make any progress at all, I felt my optimism fade.

I returned to Mili and told my parents about my lack of success.

"You need to speak to..." said my father, searching for a name that was buried deep in the fog of memory. "Captain... Manoli!" He clapped his hands and smiled.

"Who is he?"

"Captain Manoli? I met him years ago. When the Germans came, he came to my village to find food. He was poor, like all of us at the time. I supported him and his family with vegetables, olive oil, bread, and flour for the duration of the occupation. I remember him telling me he worked for a merchant marine company. He will help you."

I wasn't sure myself, but I was in no position to say no. "Where can I find him?"

"Ah," my father said. "That I do not know. But if he's still a sailor, someone in Piraeus will know him."

I returned to Athens and started my search. Piraeus was home to hundreds of shipping firms employing tens of thousands of sailors. The odds were overwhelmingly against me. I wasn't just looking for one man in a crowd of thousands; I was hoping that when I found him—if I found him—he would be willing and able to help me. It was the wildest, most ridiculous thing I had ever done, but it was a plan. And it was the only plan I had.

I went back to doing what I knew best: knocking on doors and trying to persuade strangers to help me. I spent days getting nowhere. But then I had a breakthrough.

The offices of the Livanos Shipping Company were suitably impressive for a firm with its reputation. Livanos was one of the best-known names in the merchant marine industry at that time, and it was obvious from the way the receptionist looked at me when I walked in that they were used to dealing with high-level businessmen, not scrappy seventeen-year-olds.

"Good morning," I said, flashing my brightest smile. "This is a beautiful office."

She stared. Her face was stone.

"My name is George Evangelos Danis, and I am looking for a Captain Manoli. I am hoping that—"

"He's busy," she shot back, her eyes boring into mine.

I was shocked that she'd heard of him and excited that I might even have stumbled across the right man. But I had to keep those emotions to myself. This woman was tough, and she had no intention of helping me.

"I understand," I said. "But I really would like to see him. It's important." She shook her head, her stone-faced expression not changing at all. "My father and Captain Manoli were friends, and that's why I'm here. My father sent me. Please, Miss. Can you just ask if he'll see me?"

She was about to shake her head again but hesitated just long enough for me to know that I had the smallest of breakthroughs. I smiled again, and she stood up from her desk and disappeared through a door at the back of the room.

My heart started to race as I waited. I focused on my breathing, rehearsing yet again the speech that I'd spent the previous week crafting.

Two minutes later the door opened and the receptionist came back through, followed by a well-dressed man wearing the nicest pair of shoes I'd ever seen. I was about to start my speech when he held out a hand.

"You're Evangelos Ntanis's (Danis's) boy? You look just like him! How is he?"

He took me by the shoulder and brought me to his office—a room that was beautifully furnished.

He asked me to sit down in one of the most luxurious chairs that I've ever seen and asked me what I wanted to drink.

"Water," I said shyly. He then summoned the receptionist to bring me a glass of water, and I began to feel a great weight slipping from my shoulders. We talked a while about my father and what he'd done for the captain in his time of need. Then came the question that sparked my nerves all over again.

"What are you doing here, George?"

My tongue felt heavy and dry, but I did my best to explain. I told him about my years of schooling and all the summers that I'd spent on the schooner.

He frowned. I wasn't sure if it was a good sign that he was thinking seriously about what I was saying or if it meant that I was rapidly running out of luck. "Where do you want to go?"

"America? But anywhere really. I just want a job."

"And you've got your paperwork?"

I pulled out the copy of my Seaman's Book, the official accreditation that would allow me to work on international freighters, even though I didn't have a passport. "Yes, Captain."

"And when do you want to go?"

"Anytime! I'm ready right now."

Captain Manoli nodded. "Okay." He then started to make calls.

The captain was as good as his word, and he quickly secured me a job working in the engine room on board the *Atlantic Sea*. The ten-thousand-ton boat, a liberty ship built by the Americans during World War II, was soon to be shipping fertilizer from Germany to Japan, with a plan to head to the west coast of America after that.

I had a few days to say my goodbyes to my family and friends. It was the most difficult time that I had encountered up to that point in my life. My parents, especially my mother, were crying. I promised that I would return, but my mother feared that she would never see me again—just as my grandmother never saw her son again after he emigrated to Philadelphia. I was young and full of dreams, but my parents were getting older, and the fear of the family separation for my parents was sharp.

For my readers, I know many of us have had the same experience of family moving across our large country. A lot of us have hoped to keep family close, to be able to see them often, to offer help, to learn from each other, to remain connected with our ancestors, and to build community together. But, as my parents understood, you cannot hold an adventurous child back. You simply have to send them out and learn to trust that all will be well.

I returned to Athens after all the family emotion and reported to the office, where I met some of the other crew members. We traveled together to the port of Patras to catch the ferry to Italy and made the long train journey north to the port of Bremen.

Ten years had passed since the end of the Second World War, but I was struck by the destruction that remained. As I was traveling north through Germany, I saw shells of bombed out buildings in every city. And as I was looking out, I reflected on the years during the German occupation of Greece. I could still feel some of the fear I experienced when I saw the German soldier break my friend's arm. But as I looked out on the devastation—with so many buildings totally disintegrated and plenty more left damaged beyond repair—I wondered about the cost to the German people as well.

The port itself just north of Bremen was nothing like Piraeus. And as soon as I saw the *Atlantic Sea*, all thoughts of the past vanished. I had seen plenty of big ships in Piraeus, and probably some that were bigger, but it was a little overwhelming to look up at a vessel as big as that and to know

George E. Danis

that I was in some way responsible for a journey that would take it all the way around the world.

That feeling of being out of my depth stayed with me as I went aboard and met the rest of the crew. Most of them were Greek, and they were friendly and very helpful, but they were all seasoned sailors who had spent years at sea. They looked at me and saw me for what I was: an eighteen-year-old first-timer with a lot to learn.

Fortunately, one of the old-timers, the engineering manager, took us under his wing as we spent a few days preparing to embark. His name was Panayotis, though he was so much older and had so much experience that everyone called him Captain Panayotis. He was my guide and my guru, talking to me about everything from the right way to arrange my bunk to the perils of visiting the kind of bars frequented by prostitutes an eighteen-year-old could get in trouble with.

After a week we were ready to leave. We were immediately thrown about on the North Sea and headed south toward the channel—the narrow strait that separates England from France. The closer we got, the worse the conditions became. The winds picked up, the waves surged, and despite her size, the *Atlantic Sea* started to pitch and roll like we were in a hurricane.

Right in the middle of the English Channel, when the seas were at their most violent, our antenna snapped off, leaving us without radio. Replacing it was an urgent priority, but instead of handing the job to one of the veteran sailors, it fell to me—the youngest and least experienced by far—to take on the task.

I could have said no, and as I stood on deck and looked up at the fifty-foot mast I would have to climb while the storm battered us and the ship lurched one way, then another, a part of me wished that someone else might step forward at the last moment and volunteer. But there was another voice within me, one that was louder and clearer. It said that if the crew were prepared to trust me, who was I to disagree and disappoint them? It said that I was ready for a challenge like this. It said that if I backed out now, I'd regret it.

The way up to the top of the mast was simple but terrifying. I was given a tool belt filled with wrenches, ropes, and bolts, handed the spare antenna, and told to clip it onto the belt.

"Up you go," said the sailor who had taken charge of the operation.

"How?"

He pointed at the base of the mast. There, lying at the end of a long coil of rope, was a narrow wooden seat that looked as though it had been taken from a child's swing. I stepped in, gripped the ropes, and felt myself hoisted up away from the deck.

I'd known fear before. The German soldiers in Karystos were the villain in so many of my childhood nightmares. I knew what it felt like to wake up, heart racing, head fogged, and mouth frozen with fright. But this was something else entirely. This wasn't fear. This was terror—pure, uncontainable terror.

The motion of the ship as it pitched and rolled on the waves was magnified as I swung like a pendulum above the deck. The wind drove biting rain into my face, and my fingers started to turn numb. One moment I was flying wildly out away from the mast, and the next I was hurtling back toward it, bracing for impact. I wanted to close my eyes and make it go away, but there was another part of me that was thrilled by it all. There I was, just one small slip away from falling to my death, feeling completely alive. I took a risk and looked down at the ship way below and the gnarling ocean crashing over the gunwales. It was a mistake I didn't repeat again.

When I eventually reached the top, the men were shouting to me from the deck, but the wind swept their words away like feathers. I gripped the mast with both my legs and one arm in an attempt to hold myself in place, then used my free arm to remove what was left of the old antenna. It took all my strength to put the new antenna in place and hold it there while I clamped it tight. It was a struggle, and I felt as if I was locked in an epic battle against not just the storm and the waves below but the stubborn bolts and the little rope swing that was doing its best to throw me off.

I don't know how many minutes it took to fix the antenna, but when it was over and I was being lowered back down to the deck—desperately gripping the mast to avoid swinging out again—I was exhausted, frozen numb, and faint. For the first time in all the months I'd spent at sea, I wanted to throw up. But I heard the sailors clapping, and I knew I had done well.

Working in the engine room was nowhere near as terrifying or as dangerous as replacing the antenna, but it was the hardest work I had ever carried out. The air was thick like mud, and combined with the heat and the smell of oil and fuel that covered every surface, it was enough to make even the strongest stomach feel ill. I never fully got used to it, but I learned to endure my long shifts. I focused on the tasks that I was given, worked as hard as I could to do them perfectly, and reminded myself that I was on the *Atlantic Sea* so that I could achieve my goal of reaching the United States. Long hours down in the engine room were simply the price I had to pay.

There were thirty-five crew on board, and each of them had their own way of coping with sea life. Some would spend their free time reading, others playing cards and laughing. For the cook—a red-eyed Russian who was all skin and bones—the only way he could cope was to drink a whole bottle of vodka each day. All of them had something to teach me about what was required on board, but I found myself particularly drawn to a fellow Greek named Dimitri. Like me, he was from a small village, but his mind was full of grand plans just waiting to be fulfilled. We would talk about America together, both of us adding detail and color to our dreams of what lay ahead.

It took us forty-five days to sail from the northern port of Bremen, down through the middle Atlantic to the straits

George E. Danis

of Gibraltar, and east in the Mediterranean Sea on to Cairo. After the destruction of Germany, Cairo felt like home. The streets were narrow and full of noise, just like Athens, and the food transported me all the way back to Karystos: succulent lamb rubbed with spices cooked over smoking coals, peppers and tomatoes full of flavor, coffee so strong and bitter it could bring tears to a first-timer's eyes. I liked Cairo immediately, especially as after my triumph with the antenna I was treated as an equal by the other men. I was one hundred and forty-five pounds, six feet tall, and just eighteen, but as I strolled into the city alongside my crewmates, I felt like a giant of a man.

There were differences between Cairo and Athens too. The women were shyer and more reserved than their sisters in Greece, and there were plenty of unwritten rules that Captain Panayotis had to remind me and some of the others to follow. Chief among them was this: as we moved about the city at night, it was vital that we stayed together as a pack.

When our time in Cairo was nearly over, a few of us went out for a meal one evening. There was plenty to make my young eyes stare and my imagination run free. At the end, when we were all drinking thick, potent coffee and a few of the men were smoking hookahs, a man approached. He was unremarkable looking, and I guessed he was just another Cairo local looking for an opportunity to make an easy buck from the visiting sailors.

"Gentlemen," he announced. "Please, your coffee cups. Turn them over, and I will read the grains for you."

I was brought up to have a healthy skepticism of fortune tellers, mystics, and the like, but my crewmates were different. They all eagerly tipped their coffee grains onto their saucers and listened attentively while the man went around to each one. After a few moments of staring, with a mock-serious expression on his face, he would deliver his verdict.

"You are to live a long life," he would say to one.

"This bodes well for you. You shall have great riches," he would say to another, his face locked in a smile as wide as the Nile.

"Ah! You will have children who will achieve wonderful things!"

It was all predictable and unimaginative, and everyone was laughing along, not taking it seriously. Until he reached my friend Dimitri, who was sitting right next to me.

As the man looked at Dimitri's coffee grains, his face lost its smile.

"Be careful," he said. "There are problems ahead. And soon. In the next few weeks."

Dimitri was older than me, and he was clearly troubled by what he heard. His face lost its color, and he looked nervously around the table.

I didn't like the way this cheap entertainer was manipulating us all, so I spoke up. "What are you talking about?"

He glanced at me, then looked away. "I don't want to say too much."

We left Cairo a day or two later and continued our journey through the Suez Canal. As an engineer I was fascinated by the fact that a project of that scale was almost one hundred years old. I spent the length of it—all hundred and twenty miles—lost in a daydream about how they constructed it without any of the modern tools we relied upon.

Once we were in the Indian Ocean, the weather changed. It wasn't as bad as the English Channel, but the waves were big enough for the order to go round that whenever we were on deck, all crew needed to be harnessed to a safety rope.

I was down in the engine room when I heard the alarm sound. A while later one of the crew came in and told us what had happened. A large wave crashed over the deck. One crewman wasn't wearing his harness. He was swept overboard and hurled into the sea. There was no chance of a rescue.

"Who was it?" I asked.

"Dimitri."

A heavy sadness hung over us for the rest of our trip to Japan. It was shocking to me to lose a new friend like Dimitri so suddenly. His memory stayed with me for some time.

We arrived in Osaka, Japan, and my head was spinning. The level of destruction in Germany was striking, but in Japan it was breathtaking. It wasn't just the buildings and the infrastructure that bore the scars of war. The people themselves were the most wretched and impoverished that I had ever seen. As we opened up the hull and stepped back to allow the twenty or thirty workers on board to unload the ten thousand tons of phosphate, I couldn't stop staring.

The men—none of whom were wearing anything more than old, stained loincloths—were stick thin. Their bones were jutting out from beneath skin that was stretched so tight it looked like it might burst. To my eyes they were the sorriest, weakest looking bunch of workers possible, and I doubted they would be able to fill and lift even one of the empty cloth sacks they carried, let alone repeat the act for days on end.

I was wrong. Though they were clearly malnourished and many of them were shadows of the men they had been before the war, they were the strongest, best organized, and most hardworking crew I have ever seen. They attacked the mountain of phosphate cargo in the hull of the ship with all the energy they could muster. Nobody slacked, nobody slowed. Every single worker pushed himself to maintain the frantic pace from the moment they started until the moment their supervisor gave the order to stop for lunch. Then, all those exhausted bodies would retrieve their wooden lunch boxes, eat the serving of rice and morsel of fish inside, and collapse on the ground for a few precious minutes until they were ordered to begin again.

It took them three solid weeks working at this pace: twelve hours with three shifts each day. As someone who thought they had a good work ethic, I was stunned. I never saw a single one of them get distracted or lose focus. They were phenomenal. Inspirational. As I stared at them, covered in sweat and phosphate, lungs bursting, and limbs frantically working, I was inspired. What more could I be capable of if I learned to work like this?

Just as in Cairo, we spent our free time in the city. There were no fortune tellers waiting for us, but there were many more prostitutes trying to lure us into the bars where they were working. Some of our peers would go inside, and like everything in the city, the prices charged were low. I was happy enough to go out every night to restaurants and bars and nightclubs, always grateful to have Captain Panayotis on hand to remind us of the dangers of that particular trap and protect us from getting into real trouble. He reminded us that the country had been banned from international trade until recently and that millions of people were on the verge of starvation. They were desperate, locked in a struggle for their very survival.

Like in Germany, my time in Japan left me thinking about the war. It was impossible not to reflect on the great scale of devastation and destruction. We must never forget that war is catastrophic to the human race. I believe any candidate for president should have to serve in the Armed Forces, as it is the only way to appreciate the consequences of sending young men and women into harm's way.

Until I started my time on the *Atlantic Sea,* all I knew of the war was what I'd experienced at home. I knew it to be brutal and terrifying, and I had always assumed that war was a case of weak versus strong, of winners standing tall over losers. I saw it through a child's eyes, as a matter of *them* and *us,* nothing more. In Japan, as a man, I learned more about the country's recent history. I learned about Pearl Harbor, Hiroshima, and Nagasaki. I learned about the way the Japanese fought, the way their leaders resisted surrender, and the scale of destruction unleashed by America's decision to use nuclear weapons not once, but twice.

It left a deep impression on me, a sense that in war there are no real winners and losers. In war, the leaders make their decisions—some reckless, some noble—but it is the people who must suffer the consequences. It is the people who pay the price and not just during the fighting, either. The war was a decade in the past, but as I stared at the bombed-out buildings and the broken people, it was clear that their suffering would continue for many more years.

The ancient Greeks were the first people to create a democracy. We need it more than ever today. We—the ordinary citizens who pay the taxes, who fight in the wars, and who must suffer the consequences when things go wrong—need to participate fully in the democratic process. That means voting, of course, but I believe it also means that we should communicate with our elected officials on a continuous basis. We need to be known, and the way to be known is to serve our country. If we don't serve, we are removed from the actual decisions and policies that are detrimental and catastrophic to our citizens, our country, and the world over.

In most democratic countries around the world, the citizens participate and serve their country. Then, and only then, are you a full citizen—otherwise, you are just an occupier. It is like being a tenant instead of owning your own home: with ownership comes sacrifice and responsibility.

We need our voices to be heard in actions, deeds, and participation by serving our country. We need our leaders to know that we hold them accountable. Democracy is not a matter of showing up every two years and casting our votes. Democracy is what happens when we all contribute, and we all listen. It's an ideal, and like ideals, it is never perfect. But we can strive. We can do better. For all our sakes, we must do better.

# CHAPTER FIVE
# INTO AMERICA

IT TOOK FORTY-FIVE DAYS to sail from Osaka to Oakland, California. The weather was torturous and the ship was empty and light, which meant it was rolling across the heavy Pacific waves. My shift was four to eight in the morning and the same in the afternoon. After the first shift, I would have breakfast and do maintenance and repairs in the engine room.

In those weeks we crossed the Pacific, but we might as well have traveled through space itself. We left behind the brutal poverty and trauma of Japan and emerged in a world that was utterly different in almost every respect. Sailing under the Golden Gate Bridge was a striking reminder that we were now in a land of wealth and progress, a country that seemed to me at the time to be focused purely on its own progress, not weighed down with any baggage from the past. In time I would see a different side of America. I would understand the complexity of her history and the wounds beneath the surface. But back then, in the final weeks of 1955, America was a land where the future was being created before your very eyes.

I was excited to finally arrive at the destination I had spent almost six months sailing toward and several years dreaming of. I was a little dazed as we edged into the shipyard in Oakland but snapped out of it when I heard someone with a bullhorn shouting up in Greek from the dock below.

"Is anyone on board from Evia? From Karystos?"

The man was walking up and down, repeating himself over and over.

I leaned over the rail. "Yes!" I yelled when he was close to me. "I am from Karystos!"

The man stopped and stared at me, his eyes squinting as I towered above him.

"What's your name?"

"Danis. My father is Evangelos Ntanis."

He shook his head. "I don't know that name. Do you know anyone by the name of Novas?"

"Novas? Yes! I know the family. In fact, I went to school with one of his children—Thanasis."

"Well, he is my brother!"

And so my introduction to San Francisco began.

The man with the bullhorn—Vasillis Novas—worked at the shipyard as a supervisor. He proved to be a kind, generous host. He took me and several of my shipmates under his wing, telling us where we should spend our free time during our stay in Oakland and San Francisco. The *Atlantic Sea* needed routine maintenance, as well as to be cleaned and painted, so our days were busy. But we took Vasillis's advice as much as we could, stepping wide-eyed out onto the streets of San Francisco.

It was everything I hoped it would be. It was more developed and advanced than Bremen, Cairo, or Osaka, and the cars were more luxurious than any I'd ever seen before. It was the people who really impacted me. As I watched them stroll along well-proportioned sidewalks, interacting politely with each other and looking impeccably groomed and perfectly happy with their lives, it seemed to me that I'd just landed in paradise.

Vasillis Novas didn't just offer tour advice; he also invited us many times to visit him and his family for a Sunday dinner. After so long away from home, it was a rare treat to sit around a family table and eat steaks that were bigger than both my hands combined. To see a man who had traveled from the very same corner of my homeland so settled and happy in America was inspiring. It satisfied my heart as much as the meat satisfied my senses. There I was, sitting in a comfortable house in a prosperous neighborhood, listening to Vasillis and his wife and daughter talk about everyday things like school, shopping, where they might take their next vacation, how much they enjoyed neighborhood barbecues, and the importance they placed on the local Greek Orthodox church community. I was a little spellbound. Their life was full of regular Greek things that were so familiar to me, and Vasillis appeared able to transplant them all seamlessly into a new life in America. Vasillis was both Greek and American. Both identities could coexist—even thrive—together. Sitting in that house, I felt like I was glimpsing a version of my own future as a Greek-American. I liked it a lot and hoped one day to be in the same position myself.

It was Christmastime, and Vasillis invited all of us to a party hosted by a prominent member of the local Greek community. The others bundled into taxis, but Vasillis arranged to pick me up in his car and drive me to the party himself.

I hadn't thought anything of it when he suggested he and I travel to the party together, but as soon as I stepped into his car, I could tell that he had something on his mind. Vasillis was usually loud and full of laughter, but as we drove away from the shipyard, he barely said a word.

"Tell me," he said when we were clear of the docks. "Have you ever thought about jumping ship? Maybe staying here, in the Bay Area?"

Immediately, I was aware of the fact that there were two different answers within me: there was the truth, and then there was the wise response that would save me from a whole world of trouble. Jumping ship wasn't just controversial and against the terms of my employment; it was illegal. As sailors we were allowed to be in each country we visited only while our ship was in port. To jump ship was to become an illegal alien. It was a crime. If I disappeared from Oakland and people suspected that Vasillis himself had played a part in it, he would be lucky to keep his job.

"No," I said. "I wouldn't do something like that."

Vasillis dropped the topic, and we carried on to the party. It was a lavish evening in a beautiful house, with steaks and ribs and all kinds of other great food. The other guests at the party were all elegantly dressed, and I'd never been surrounded by so much wealth, especially not when almost everyone in the room was Greek. But, unlike in Karystos, where the elites looked down on poor people like me, there was no sense of my being out of place or not welcome. People were friendly and easy to talk to, and plenty of them encouraged me to consider making America my permanent home one day. Just as I had in the car, I was careful to not give anything away, so I just thanked them for their kindness and smiled warmly.

Our host was yet another George—George Christopher—and he would go on to serve two terms as mayor of San Francisco and face off against Ronald Reagan in an unsuccessful bid to secure the Republican nomination for governor of California. Back in Christmas 1955, our host was already an accomplished, successful man, and his home was a clear demonstration of just how far he'd come. I enjoyed all the time I spent in the company of Vasillis and his family, but this was something else entirely.

Vasillis Novas showed me that it was possible to recreate the warmth of home here in America, but George Christopher showed me how much further my innate ambition could take me in the United States compared to back in Greece. I could live in America and still enjoy all the aspects of the Greek community that I loved while at the same time benefiting from the opportunities and potential for success that the country itself embraced. I could leave my homeland and find myself in an even better version of home—one without the old prejudices, the legacy of war, or the instability of politics.

When Vasillis Novas asked me on the drive to the party whether I'd ever considered jumping ship, I lied and told him no. The truth was that I had thought about it a lot, but I had yet to make a plan. After a few hours in the company of George Christopher and the rest of the Greek community of San Francisco and beyond, however, I decided: I was going to jump ship. And I was going to do it soon. Just not yet.

It was early January when the captain announced that the *Atlantic Sea* had been commissioned to spend the rest of the year ferrying scrap metal between North America, Japan, and Europe. It was time to leave Oakland, and there was a collective sense of sadness among the crew. It had been a wonderful three-and-a-half weeks in the company of the San Francisco Greek community, but now it was over.

For me, the sadness of saying goodbye was lessened knowing that I would return to America again one day. Everything I had seen reinforced my confidence in the place, but it also showed me that I wasn't ready. Even though I was nineteen and happy to work alongside the other men on board, I wasn't quite ready to take the risk of jumping ship.

Within days of leaving, we were thrown into bad weather and rough seas—seas so rough that the vodka-marinated cook was unable to serve up anything much more than cold tins of beans. There was little time to think about the good times we left behind, let alone how I might engineer a return to the United States. With the ship being hurled around

George E. Danis

again, all we could do was hope that the worst would soon be behind us.

For months we shuttled back and forth across the Pacific: San Pedro, California; Osaka; San Diego; and back. It was a tough assignment, and it got tougher when we discovered that we were going to stop shipping scrap metal and move on to shipping grain to Poland. This new cargo required a change to the ship's hold, with us constructing huge wooden partitions so that wheat would stay in one place and not risk destabilizing the ship as it slid from one side to the other.

Making these alterations was a big job, and it fell to us crewmen to do it as we sailed from Osaka to Vancouver. The men were not happy about the extra work, especially because there was no increase in our pay or overtime for the extra work we would do. They griped and grouched about how someone ought to go and confront the captain, but nobody volunteered.

I figured that it was an important task and one that was worth risking the captain's anger. So I told them I'd do it.

They weren't sure that I was serious at first, but nobody else wanted to step up, so they agreed to send me.

Walking to the captain's cabin was nowhere near as terrifying as being hoisted up to change the antenna in the middle of the storm. In fact, as I prepared to deliver my speech about how the crew wanted to have their extra work recognized with extra pay, I felt perfectly calm. There was nothing to fear, and everything to gain.

I knocked on the door and waited.

When he finally emerged, the captain looked at me as though he'd never seen me before. "What do you want?"

I delivered my speech. I kept it brief, allowing just enough eye contact to appear sincere, but not so much that I looked belligerent. I finished with a nod and a smile, hoping that we could conclude our business quickly.

The captain's expression was stone. Then he slammed the door in my face.

I returned to the crew mess and told them what happened. They were disappointed, and I was embarrassed. We all sat around like that, moping and griping more than ever, until the door opened and the captain walked in.

He did not like what he saw. "What are you doing sitting around like this? Get back to work."

The men were equally upset. Pretty soon the room was full of yelling on both sides. Thankfully, the captain saw sense soon enough, and the next day we were working on the partitions, happy with the knowledge that we were all getting paid extra for it.

From Vancouver we headed south into a very angry Pacific Ocean. The waves were pounding the ship and landing on the deck with such violent crashes that it sounded as if we would break apart and sink at any moment. But in time the waves eased, and we made it to the Panama Canal—a truly extraordinary feat of engineering that allowed us to skip right through to the Atlantic. Within about thirty days we were navigating the rivers and locks of Germany that led us to Poland.

There I experienced yet another dose of culture shock, as I saw for the first time what life was like in a communist country. Some of it was just as I'd imagined it would be, with gray buildings and sparse shops, but there were parts of Poland that caught me by surprise: the people were not miserable or suspicious of us. Instead, I found them to be warm and friendly, and I had many good evenings out in the city of Gdańsk, eating and drinking with three or four other crewmates for less than five dollars total, laughing and dancing with the locals.

With the ship empty of grain we set sail again. This time we headed back to the United States, but toward the East Coast instead of the west. We'd stop briefly in Norfolk, Virginia, to load up with grain, then return across the Atlantic to Gibraltar, across the eastern Mediterranean Sea, north to the Aegean Sea, then through the Dardanelles and the Black Sea to Odessa in the USSR. I had no problem with the idea of returning to the world of communist rule, but I also had no intention of being there. As far as I was concerned, Norfolk, Virginia, was the perfect opportunity to put my plan into action. It was time for me to jump ship.

As well as feeling just a little older than I had in Oakland, the main reason for me wanting to jump ship on the East Coast was the fact that it was close to my family. My uncle—the one who had been sending wonderful gifts over for years—was still living in Philadelphia, and my mother's cousin was living in the Boston area. I had an open invitation from both sets of relatives to go and live and work among them. I'd spent many weeks trying to work out which one would be better and eventually decided that Boston was the best option. Early on during my time on the *Atlantic Sea,* I told plenty of people on board about my uncle in Philly. If anyone did decide to investigate my disappearance and got one of my crewmates to talk, I'd be easy to find, and my uncle would end up in trouble.

I had to be careful every step of the way, especially as I knew that there were two other crewmen who were planning to jump ship as well. Back in the early days of my time on board the *Atlantic Sea,* when I'd been loose with my tongue and talked about my uncle in Philly, I also mentioned my desire to live in America one day to a few people. When two of them told me that they intended to jump ship—one heading to New Jersey, the other to New York—I let my guard down and told them I was planning on doing likewise. I innocently assumed there would be safety in numbers, and that if three of us were all planning on leaving together, nothing could go wrong.

By the time we arrived in Norfolk, Virginia, I was starting to regret going public with my plans. But I was committed now, and turning my back on the other two would only arouse their suspicions and surely make matters worse for me. So the three of us spent our free time wandering around Norfolk together, taking a little extra time at the train station as we figured out how we could reach our own ultimate destinations.

A day or two before the ship was due to leave for Odessa— and a couple of days after we were paid—we made our move.

We sauntered off toward the dock early one evening, leaving everything but our wallets, Seaman's Book, and the clothes on our backs behind on the ship. When we were sure nobody was following us, we headed for the station and vanished into the night.

I panicked as I discovered it wasn't as easy as I'd imagined it would be to get a train to Boston without knowing where and how things work, especially the train schedules. I arrived in New York City without understanding English, and constantly looking over my shoulder for immigration officers was a nightmare. I spent my first night sleeping at some corner of the station. The next day, using the English dictionary I brought with me, I managed to read the train schedules. I was so happy when I found the Boston train and got on it without being apprehended by the immigration officers.

There was snow on the ground when my train pulled into Boston's South Station, but the welcome I received from my extended family was warm enough to melt the rail tracks. I'd never met my mother's cousins before, but they embraced me as their own and hurried me back to their home in Belmont, west of the city.

I'd been plagued with nerves ever since leaving the *Atlantic Sea,* becoming increasingly paranoid with every stranger who looked at me and every police officer I encountered on the twenty-four-hour journey north. I felt like I was wearing a sign around my neck that said *ILLEGAL IMMIGRANT* and that anybody looking at me could tell that I didn't belong in

America. I tried to make myself invisible behind my magazine, but at the same time kept a watchful eye on everybody around me. I studied everyone and planned a possible escape route in case things went wrong. It was exhausting.

As soon my journey was over and I stepped into the home of Alex and Katherine Paraskos, I relaxed. I was out of sight of the authorities and once again back in the embrace of my Greek family. Greece was an ocean away, but I was finally home.

It didn't take long for me to settle into family life. Uncle Alex owned a restaurant near their home, and I immediately joined the team, bussing tables, washing dishes, and making coffee. But with five people already working for him and the restaurant only big enough for twenty customers at a time, my time there was always going to be short. Immigration authorities made a habit of checking family-run restaurants, especially Greek and Italian places. Whatever task I did in that little restaurant, I was visible. And since my English was still poor, I was liable to attract the wrong kind of attention. I was too much of a risk to everyone.

The solution emerged quickly. One of Uncle Alex's friends worked for The Town Diner, another Greek-owned local restaurant. Jim Lemonias was a short-order cook at the diner, where they were always understaffed. He knew my older brothers from his time in Karystos and was happy to recommend me to his boss, a man that most people only ever called Mr. Contos. Like me, Mr. Contos was born in Greece and moved to the United States in his early twenties. Unlike me, he was fully legal, and over the years he had developed his business interests well.

I started work at Mr. Contos's diner one week after I arrived in Boston. The diner was run by his oldest son, George, and his son-in-law, Chris. I was assigned to Jim in the kitchen and the front grill, where I was given the usual first-timer tasks, which included filling in for the dishwasher on Fridays, clearing floors, and helping the cooks without getting in the way. It was simple work, and with the heat and time pressures, it was not too different from the engine room of the *Atlantic Sea*. Best of all, the kitchen had a basement, far from public view. When I was down there, I felt protected.

Jim had also arranged for me to rent a room from an Armenian family. It was on the top floor of a building on Dexter Avenue, just a short walk from the diner. There was a Greek Orthodox church nearby, and I went there the very first Sunday. I met the priest afterward—a smiling, warm-hearted man named Father Emanuel Metaxas—and happily accepted his invitation to return to his house for lunch that very day.

In just over two weeks, I went from feeling nervous about jumping ship to landing myself a job, a home, and a community of fellow Greeks and loving family. It couldn't have gone better.

My experience of the Greek community in Watertown and in the Boston area was overwhelming. The priest and members of the Greek community who I met supported Greek Americans from every walk of life. Everyone offered acceptance and welcome, especially Jim Lemonias and his whole family.

Jim took me under his wing and included me in every family gathering, as if I were one of his brothers. Jim had five sisters and one brother, and at his sister Georgia's wedding, I was a part of the wedding party. I felt like I had a second family in Watertown, and I owe a debt of gratitude to the whole Lemonias family. They were my mentors when I was here alone.

On the evening of the rehearsal dinner, after we had finished up at the church, we were all invited to a dinner at the house. It was almost midnight when we finished eating, and I decided to walk home as it was less than a mile. I was on Second and Third Street when a car slowed behind me. I looked, saw that it was a police car with two officers in it, and started running.

"Stop!" one of them shouted. I carried on running. Then one of them fired his gun into the air, and I did exactly what I was told.

"Put your hands in the air!"

I obeyed instantly.

"We've had reports of a peeping Tom," said one of the officers as he approached. "What are you doing out this late?"

"I was at my friend's house for a wedding rehearsal dinner."

"Oh? Whose house?"

"Jim Lemonias," I said, trying to sound as authentically American as possible.

They looked skeptical and told me to get in the car and

direct them to Jim's house.

Jim was still up when we got there and happily backed up my story. It also helped that both cops were regulars at the diner, and they soon offered to drive me back to my room. I gladly accepted, but I felt nervous all the way home.

It wasn't my only close call with the police, and Jim wasn't my only source of support in the Greek community. A neighbor called Steve offered to drive me to my second job in Boston, where I worked from 7:00 a.m. to 3:00 p.m. in the kitchen of a restaurant called Star Lunch. Steve was working similar hours nearby, and at the end of my shift, he'd come by the restaurant and sit and have a few drinks with the owner.

Those were different times, and Steve would think nothing of getting into the cab of his truck after sharing a whole bottle of vodka. He'd drive pretty well, but he'd be puffing on a cigar and filling the whole cab with smoke.

One time when we were driving through Harvard Square, Steve ran a red light. A police siren sounded, and Steve pulled over.

"Watch this," he said, taking a long draw on his cigar.

The officer knocked on the window, which Steve wound down. He then blew his lungful of smoke right into the officer's face.

"I'm sorry for missing that sign, Officer," said Steve. "It's kind of hard to see in here with all this smoke."

The officer nodded. "I'll just let you off with a warning, then."

Twenty years later, after a night out watching baseball with some friends, I stopped by a diner called the New Yorker. It was 2:00 a.m., but the place was busy, with a long line snaking back from the counter. I went to the front to ask how long we'd have to wait and saw my friend Steve standing there, puffing away on a cigar.

"Mr. Danis!" he yelled. "Your table is ready!"

It was a great and unexpected reunion.

Mr. Contos's diner was a goldmine because there were two large manufacturing plants nearby. One was the Arsenal factory, manufacturing military products, and the other was Hood Rubber, making rubber tires. The workers provided Mr. Contos with a steady flow of hungry customers. Each day the diner was full at breakfast, lunch, and even until it closed at 2:00 a.m., when the shifts changed. With that much demand on the kitchen staff, I was soon promoted to short-order cook on the night shift. I went from helping and cleaning the kitchen to cooking hamburgers, scrambled eggs, pancakes, omelets, and the rest.

Even better was the fact that the job came with a fifteen-dollar-per-week increase. I was now earning seventy-five dollars a week—all paid in cash under the table, of course—and I was almost completely happy. The one problem was the fact that the short-order grill wasn't located down in the basement, far from view. It was up in the main restaurant, in full view of all the diners. Still, I figured that immigration officials had better things to do than go trawling diners for illegals in the dead of night. As long as I kept my head down and my mouth shut, I hoped I'd be okay.

Most of the time my approach worked. But every once in a while I found myself attracting more attention than I wanted, like the evening when a guy came in and slumped down at the counter in front of my grill. It was way past midnight, and the diner was filling up with workers ending their shift at the local armory or all the bars in the area that had closed.

"I want an omelet with a dozen eggs," sighed the man. "And twelve slices of toast." He looked tired from his shift at a bar, but even so I was surprised. Like every other Greek I knew, I was taught to savor my food, not shovel it down in obscene quantities as this guy wanted to do. After all, the pleasure in eating is to be found before swallowing, not after, why hurry?

"Are you sure?" I asked. "That's a lot of food."

The guy stared at me, perfectly still, as if he was so hungry he was chewing on my words already.

"Make me the omelet, you goddamn Greek," he snarled. "And don't forget my twelve slices of toast!"

I did what he asked, made the food, and did my best to keep out of his way while he hunched over his plate and ate.

"Give me another one," he snapped once his plate was empty.

This time I didn't question him at all but quietly made and served the giant omelet.

His eating pace slowed, and he was clearly struggling to make it all the way through, but he didn't give up. Only when he finished and paid the check did he show any sign of the inevitable pain that must have been mounting in his guts.

He slumped forward, head on the counter. The whole diner could hear his groaning, which was getting louder by the second.

Soon, he was lying on the floor, as sick as a dog.

From the tables near the front, a diner called out, "Somebody should call the police."

"They're on their way!" said one of the waitresses.

I felt the panic grip my throat. I turned my back on the diner and focused on my grill, desperately hoping that that was not going to be the day I got caught.

That night passed without incident for me, but it set me on edge. From then on I was more nervous, more cautious around diners. I tried not to speak unless I absolutely had to, knowing my accent alone was enough to give me away.

I was back at work one afternoon, enjoying my one daily luxury of a cup of coffee at the counter before my 4:00 p.m. shift began. Two well-dressed men came in and sat on either side of me. I tried to keep my focus on the cup in my hands, but I could tell they were focused purely on me. My heart was instantly racing.

Now, I'd been in Boston long enough to handle any order given to me for omelets, burgers, or whatever, but my English still wasn't particularly good. So when one of the men in suits leaned in close, pulled out his badge, and spoke to me, I struggled to understand every single word he said. But I knew enough to know that they were from the U.S. Immigration

George E. Danis

Service, and they wanted to see my papers.

I turned and smiled. "My jacket," I said, trying to make my accent sound as much like a native Bostonian as I possibly could. "Papers are in my jacket. Downstairs. I bring them now, yes?"

Both men smiled and nodded in return, and they seemed to be happy to let me leave the counter and walk back toward the stairs.

As soon as I was in the kitchen, I started running for the back exit. I exploded out the door into the late afternoon gloom, around the corner of the diner, and right into the arms of one of the men I'd just left at the counter.

"Whoa there, Skip," he said, grabbing the top of my right arm with a grip that was pure granite. "Where are you going?"

I was too scared to say anything.

His partner arrived shortly after, and within seconds I was being dragged, handcuffed, toward the back of their car.

I slumped into the back seat, terrified. I was nineteen years old, but I felt like bawling for my mother to come and save me. This was my nightmare, right here: I was about to be arrested and thrown in jail. Then who knew what else would happen to me? This was the one thing that I had been terrified of ever since I decided I wanted to live in America. This was the one thing that nobody I knew could do anything to help.

I was alone.

# CHAPTER SIX
# THE END AND THE BEGINNING

EVEN BEFORE I WAS ARRESTED, driven to Charles Street Jail, and had my clothes swapped for a prison uniform, I felt as though my life was over. I sat in the car, metal cuffs biting into my wrists, unable to escape the feeling that the hopes I had been so carefully nurturing for years were now dead.

Life inside the prison did little to change my opinion. I was placed in a section of the jail reserved for other illegal immigrants. There must have been fifty or sixty of us in there. There were no Greeks among us, but plenty of Italians, Spanish, and even a few Canadians. As I listened to the quiet hum of different languages drifting out of the cells, I felt even worse. In the months that I'd spent living under the radar, part of me started to believe that I was almost secure. But the Charles Street Jail was a clear reminder of how easy it was for the government to round up us illegals. Those months I spent living and working and enjoying my new American life had been good, and a part of me hoped that I'd be able to get away with being an illegal immigrant for years and years to come. Those full cells were a perfect reminder that my days as an illegal were numbered. Sooner or later I was always going to get caught.

I feared that nobody would remember me or be willing to fight for my release and that I was going to be left to rot in that jail. I hoped to be deported right away, but as the days inched by and none of the guards would talk to me about my case, I started to fear the worst. Thankfully, a surprise visit from Father Metaxas after I'd been in the jail several days reassured me that the friends I made had not abandoned me. He had good news for me too: Mr. Contos promised to do what he could to help.

Mr. Contos was more than just a local businessman with a diner. His success over the years was significant, and he owned a vacation home in Hyannis Port on Cape Cod, not far from a compound owned by some local political movers and shakers. I was still ignorant of American politics and knew nothing of Hyannis Port or the people who lived there, but I trusted Mr. Contos and knew that if he had agreed to help, things would surely work out well.

The days continued to inch by, as slow as the passing of a season. Father Metaxas returned for another visit and told me to keep my spirits up and trust that Mr. Contos would come through for me, but the longer I was stuck in jail, the more I struggled to keep the fear at bay.

Yet Mr. Contos was as good as his word and was working hard behind the scenes to secure my swift deportation. He made contact with the U.S. senator from Massachusetts—his

George E. Danis

Hyannis Port neighbor, Senator John F. Kennedy—and after two weeks, I was told by a guard that I had a visitor who wanted to speak with me.

The guard walked me to the interview room, and I stepped in and saw my visitor. He was older than me by a decade or more, but he had the air of a much younger man. He was a good size and athletic, more like a Greek young man than most of the Americans I had met. He looked at me carefully, then introduced himself.

"I'm Senator Kennedy," he said. It wasn't a name I'd ever heard before, but I liked the way he said it. He was confident and charismatic, and I felt some of the tension I'd been carrying ease off a little. "I hear you're from Greece."

"Yes," I said, aware of how thick my accent was compared to his. "From Karystos. It's near Athens."

He smiled. "I love Greece, especially the history, the philosophers, democracy, and classics. And the language and the literature too."

I was surprised. I'd met plenty of first- and second-generation Greek immigrants in America, and we all talked fondly and often about our love for our homeland, but this man in front of me, with his light eyes and northern complexion, was clearly not a Greek. I was intrigued. "You've read Homer?"

That was all it took. He unbuttoned his suit jacket, sat down, and launched into a long description of his favorite Greek writers and philosophers. It was like being at home with my father and mother, discussing the great legacy that our ancient ancestors left us.

Without warning, the man's expression changed slightly. He looked a little concerned. "You're not a communist, are you?"

"Not at all, sir."

"Good," he said, standing up and fastening his jacket. "I'm going to have my office help with your release. You'll have forty-five days to get your affairs in order and leave the country. You promise me you'll do that?"

"I will. Thank you."

We shook hands, and my visitor left. A guard stepped in and stared at me.

"How do you know the senator?" he asked, his voice full of amazement.

"I don't." I shrugged. It was nice to be able to talk about home like that, and I was encouraged by the idea that I would soon be out of jail and given enough time to find work on a ship that would take me back home. But I wasn't starstruck or overawed by meeting JFK. To me he was just a genuinely nice guy who had a keen interest in Greek philosophy and the classics.

The next day, the two immigration officers who had arrested me returned me to the diner. As I entered, everyone, including customers who knew me, started clapping. I went back to work that very evening, grateful for the support of friends and the kindness of strangers.

At the end of the month, I took the train to New York to find a job on a merchant ship heading for Europe. It took me more than a week of searching, but I finally found a

Portuguese freighter going to Lisbon. I also checked with my previous employer, the Livanos Ship Company, and there were no hard feelings about me jumping ship the previous year. In fact, they even sent my wages and the possessions I left behind on to my parents in Mili.

The weather was rough when we left New York but not as bad as many of the voyages I'd been on before, especially compared to the Pacific. We arrived in Portugal in about thirty days, and from there I found an Italian ship needing crew that was headed to Naples. From there I took a train to Brindisi, then got a job on a Greek ferry boat that was going back and forth between Italy and Patras. Finally, after two trips on the ferry—and three years since I had left—I was able to return home to Karystos to see my parents and my brothers.

I had a lot of time to think on the long journey home about my experience as an illegal immigrant, and I have thought more about it over the years since. In all that time, the issue of immigration in our nations has continued to remain unsolved. We are now experiencing anarchy across the southern border, and some cities are declaring a state of emergency. The political leaders in the nation's capital have been ignoring these conditions, and the suffering of the migrants has gotten worse. They shouldn't be crossing illegally, but you can't blame them for trying to cross into the United States for opportunities that are nonexistent in their homeland.

The U.S. government is in a state of total paralysis. It's ignoring both the problem of illegal migration and the benefits that we can derive from a comprehensive immigration policy. The U.S. economy will need millions of new laborers in the years to come if it is to become competitive and sustain the future of global competition. Immigration remains the most efficient way to increase our labor force. Yet we are failing to do all we can to allow us to recruit to the best of our ability.

We also need to keep our nation safe, to know who's coming in and why, yet the control of our borders is poor. Today, we find ourselves in a state of chaos. It was bad before the COVID-19 pandemic, and it is even worse now. While our leaders talk long and loud about supporting American industry, the reality is that our manufacturing sector has been thrown into disarray because of labor shortages. We've got supply-chain issues that are so great we need between six and nine million new workers in the labor market to fix the labor problems within the manufacturing sector in the United States. If leaders cannot meet that need, all their words about the American dream and American products for the future are just empty rhetoric.

This is why we as citizens need to participate and demand solutions from our government, not rhetoric and political speeches just before the next election. It is so ironic that we hear the political candidates always say they will create jobs that pay well, yet they have no idea what they are talking about. They are clueless. The United States does not have enough labor to produce the products we need now, never mind all the outsourced products that we import. And with over ten million open jobs in the United States, the holes in our labor market are huge. We need a comprehensive immigration policy now.

For the last quarter century, our lawmakers have done little to address the issue, and we have suffered as a result. They should have fixed the immigration issue, creating clear pathways for the country to recruit the workers we desperately need. They should have made the process of coming to America legally achievable and accessible for those we want to attract—so achievable and accessible that taking the illegal route no longer makes sense. We need to demand that our lawmakers do better and create new immigration laws expeditiously that are fit for purpose.

---

I arrived home and was reunited with my family. Thirty months had passed since I last saw them, and our reunion impacted me even more than I imagined it would. I was especially touched to see my little nephew, George—my brother Evangelos's first child. He was almost three, and I relished the opportunity to treat him the way my own uncle had, lavishing gifts on us brothers. I had been living very frugally in Boston, taking most of my meals at the diner, so I had about $1,800 with me—a good amount in those days. I used a few of those dollars to buy little George a tricycle in a shop in Athens.

When my nephew saw me disembarking from a small boat in the port of Karystos carrying the tricycle, he was so bashful he ran home. After hugs and welcome from my parents, my brother Evangelos and his lovely wife Josefina—called Fini for short—walked home with me. George was waiting for us. I handed the tricycle to him, and he was so excited and overwhelmed, he didn't know what to do. He hid for a while before eventually coming back, then he checked out the tricycle and covered me with hugs and kisses. All the fatigue from the long journey and the stress of being arrested and deported vanished. I was home again. Nothing else mattered.

Being back on the island was wonderful. I stayed with Evangelos, his wife—who I was meeting for the first time—and little George at their home in Karystos and walked up to Mili to see my parents every day. They were both well, and we savored the time we had together. I enjoyed hearing all the news about the village and the gossip about my friends and family—how many were still around and who was married.

But we knew our time together was short. Like every young man born in Greece, I had been drafted to serve in the military. The original call up came when I was away in the Merchant Marine, but now that I was back it was only a matter of time before I was instructed to serve.

In March 1958, I packed my bags again and began my service within the Greek Navy near Piraeus. They prepared us well with forty days of basic training—forty days of the most demanding physical activity I had ever experienced. Being woken up in the middle of the night to swim in the cold sea or run up a steep hill that appeared to have no end was not in any way fun for me. Yet, when it was over, I signed up for more of the same. I decided to apply to become a Navy frogman and join the Underwater Demolition Command (UDT) unit. I liked the idea of joining the Special Forces and testing myself against the best. And when each day was finally over and I crept, exhausted, into my bunk, I fell into a sleep that was deeper than any I had ever experienced. Joining the Navy was painful and often terrifying, but I knew that it was good for me.

Naturally, we spent a lot of time on beaches, and it was there that I learned one of the most valuable lessons of my life. Our instructor had us form a line. The person at the end then picked up a handful of sand and passed it to the person beside him, who passed it on to the next and so on. It didn't take long for all of the sand to have escaped and our instructor to start talking.

"This is what happens with orders and messages if you do not establish good models of communication," he said. "If you do not have the tools to pass information on accurately, the information will be lost."

We see this in our media today. The established press no longer appears to be committed to reporting events faithfully. Instead, they select the version of the truth that most clearly aligns with their values and will continue to boost their profitability. Social media is even worse, with little or no sense of responsibility when it comes to verifying what is shared on the platforms. We live in a world where truth is seen as fluid rather than factual, flexible rather than fixed. We live in serious times—times where democracy is under threat the world over, and our way of life can no longer be guaranteed for generations to come—yet what hope do we have when we cannot even agree on the most basic truths of all? We are standing on the beach, our hands empty apart from a few grains of sand.

It took sixty days of training before I made it onto the UDT team—sixty days of intense physical activity at all hours of the day and night. I was fit already when I started, but by the end I was in the best shape of my life. Yet upon completion of the training, I did not apply for a position that would send me back into the water or headfirst into some other physically demanding challenge in some far-flung corner of Greece. Having been away from my family so much during the previous years, I wanted to be as close to them as possible. With Alexandros and Polychronis both living and working in Athens, I decided to stay near the capital.

I applied for an administrative position at a base a few miles outside Athens. Even though I ended up spending my days behind a desk, my time was not wasted. I wasn't much of a typist, but I was no worse than any of the others on the base, so I was given the kinds of assignments that would prove to be invaluable in later life. I wrote daily status reports, learned about numerous administrative procedures, worked with spreadsheets, and saw up close how important accountability is in order for a team to function well. From my interactions with the officers, I learned a lot about the art of negotiation, too, and throughout my entire eighteen months on the base, I was aware that I was learning skills that would be of significant benefit to me.

Best of all, my job was weekdays only, which left me plenty of free time to head into Athens. I spent as much time as possible with my brother Polychronis and his wife Pagona and also restarted my door-to-door sales of cloth to the budget-conscious housewife. I was several years older than when I first did it, and I'd seen a lot more of the world. Now, being older and wiser, I added new items like bathing suits to my product line. Most women loved the new products; they were so excited that some of them would take their clothes off and try them on in front of me. But I was always very careful not to get into trouble.

All that life experience taught me a valuable lesson about the art of sales: that we are all selling all the time, whether we're applying for our education or for a new job, establishing ourselves in a new community, or trying to win over someone's affection. The ones who are the best at sales are the ones who are themselves. People can smell a fake a mile off, so being authentic and genuine is vital. Even though we usually measure the success of a sale by the amount of money it brings in, my belief is that the true measure of success for a salesperson is how much people trust them. If a salesperson is clearly putting on an act, how can that be good for anyone?

My time drafted into the Greek Navy shaped me in so many ways, and today I am increasingly convinced that it is an idea worth returning to. Imposing national service on a country's young people is a controversial move, but it is not unheard of. Sweden, Norway, Greece, and Israel are among those that currently have military service of at least nine months, and I am grateful for the opportunities that my time with the Navy outside of Athens gave me. I learned a lot of skills, but it went deeper than that. For those eighteen months, I had a clear sense of purpose, an awareness that I was contributing something of value to my homeland. For that time I was giving, not taking.

I believe that as a country we should look again at the idea of national—though not necessarily military—service. If every young man and woman spent a year-plus serving their country in a variety of sectors, the impact would be colossal. Imagine having millions of volunteers on hand each year to resource the work of FEMA, boost the efforts of nonprofits, help staff early education, help train the long-term unemployed, or provide labor for so many of the infrastructure projects this country so desperately needs. Think of the skills that those young people would acquire and the sense of purpose, community, citizenship, and responsibility that would be instilled deep within them. And what if national service like this was linked to a reduction in college tuition costs? Wouldn't that be a win-win, not to be borrowing money and having to pay it back?

While my opinion of national service has changed over the years, by the time I had been with the Navy for eighteen months I was starting to feel a burning, desperate desire to return to America. I wanted to put into practice the skills I learned on the naval base and on the streets of Athens. I wanted to get on with my life, to test myself in the only country where success seemed truly possible. But I didn't just want to earn money, I needed to. My father was well beyond retirement age, and his health was starting to deteriorate, making it difficult for him to work on the farm. With my three brothers all happily living in Greece, earning Greek wages, the idea of my achieving financial success in America and sending money home mattered more than ever.

At the time, national service in Greece lasted two and a half years, but for people like me who needed to work to support an aging father, the term was reduced to eighteen months. It took a while to gain the correct approval, but eventually I was allowed to leave in eighteen months.

Once discharged I spent some time back in Mili with my parents and set about trying to find a way back to the United States. I visited the embassy and discovered that the immigration process was going to take years, and even then, there were no guarantees. So I moved on to my alternative plan and searched for a job on board a merchant ship.

Yet again Captain Manoli—even though I left the first ship that he put me on—came through. He offered me a job on board a vessel that I hoped would eventually end up in America, though, as ever, the ship's itinerary would be decided only once it was under way, and there were no guarantees. I didn't mind so much. It was 1960, I was twenty-three years old, and finally free to start building my new life. I would head back to the western suburbs of Boston, be reunited with my friends in the Greek community, and maybe even take up my old job again in the diner.

Resting up in Mili before I said my final goodbyes and

headed back to sea, I let myself imagine what it would be like to return to Boston. I pictured the friends and the family members I would be reunited with, especially the Lemonias family and their daughter, Sia. They were so kind to me, as were the Contos family with the diner and my spiritual leader, Father Metaxas. I remembered how good it felt to be in a country where almost anything felt possible. I daydreamed about the life I might build for myself, the work I might do, and the family I would love. These were good dreams to savor, but they were not the only thoughts that filled my mind.

I guessed that, having been arrested and deported once, I was more vulnerable. I could no longer assume that I could live my life under the radar and avoid all detection. If I jumped ship again and entered America as an illegal immigrant, there was a good chance that I might end up right back where I had been before: arrested, deported, and back home in Greece.

I had a choice to make, but the choice was not about whether I stayed in Mili or returned to Boston. That much had already been decided. My choice was whether I worried about being deported again. I decided not to, pushing the thoughts out of my mind every time they threatened to enter. If I wanted my plan to succeed, I had to be prepared to struggle, to suffer, and to try again and again. The Navy taught me that on all those early morning runs up steep mountainsides where my legs burned like fire and my lungs turned to stone.

So I said my goodbyes to my parents and stood on Mili's

craggy rocks high above Karystos, taking a long, last look at the ocean that spread out into the distance. I had no idea when I would return. But it was time for me to leave. That much I knew for sure.

## CHAPTER SEVEN
# AMERICA, AGAIN

As soon as I heard the *Alexandria* was heading for Mobile, Alabama, I knew two things. First, even though it was more than a thousand miles away from my ultimate destination, I knew that I would jump ship there. Second, I knew that I would have to break my promise to keep my plans secret. If I was going to have any hope of making it back to Boston this time, I would have to rely on someone else to help me. This wasn't new—I'd taken a similar risk on the *Atlantic Sea* before and told the other two who jumped with me—but could I really hope to get away with it a second time?

My problem was money. I figured that to ride the bus all the way from Mobile, Alabama, up to my uncle's in Philly— let alone all the way back to Boston—was going to cost me at least thirty dollars. I didn't have thirty dollars. In fact, despite my hard work selling cloth in Athens, I was barely able to afford to live, so I left Greece with almost no money at all. I needed a loan, and there was only one person I could ask: Dimitri. He and I became friends ever since I arrived on board carrying a present for him from his wife, who I met at the shipping company office in Piraeus.

Dimitri agreed to the loan and offered to help me slip away from the *Alexandria*. Soon after we docked, he and I announced once evening that we were heading into Mobile to celebrate Dimitri's name day—an Orthodox tradition where those who are named after a Christian saint or martyr celebrate their name day as if it were their own birthday. We walked off the ship empty-handed, strolled away from the docks, found a restaurant, and had a few drinks celebrating his name day. We ate quickly. After that we took a taxi to the bus depot where, at a little before 8:00 p.m. on October 26, 1960, when all the light had gone from the sky and the thick rain clouds above opened up, I said thank you yet again to Dimitri. I watched him drive away in the taxi, then went to buy my ticket with the money he loaned me.

It struck me as odd how differently I felt compared to the first time I jumped ship. Five years earlier in Norfolk, Virginia, part of me was caught up in the excitement of the moment. I felt suspicious of people, but most of my nerves were focused on the train journey and whether I would be able to find the right train in New York. But at the bus station in Mobile, even though I was a good deal older and plenty wiser, I was nearly paralyzed by fear, just as I was when I watched the German soldier explode with violence back in Karystos. But instead of physical pain, what I feared now was being caught. I was aware of every person in the ticket office, trying to figure out which ones were either looking at me too much or trying too hard to appear as though they were ignoring me. I tried to make myself as inconspicuous as possible as I waited in line and kept my voice low as I ordered my ticket to Philadelphia—using my very best pronunciation.

Between the fear in my head and the hammering of the rain on the roof, it was all too intense. By the time I bought my ticket and found the right bus, all I wanted was to disappear. I made my way to the seats at the back of the bus, pulled my raincoat tight, and opened the magazine that I'd brought with me. As the bus pulled out from the station, I sank deeper into my seat. All I wanted was to be invisible for the next few hours.

We'd only just left the station when the bus slammed to a halt and paused at the side of the road. I peered down the aisle and saw the driver walking back. He was looking right at me. I tried to shrink back into my seat and hide even more of myself behind my magazine, the panic rising like bile in my throat.

The driver reached my seat and started yelling at me to get up. My head flooded. My heart surged. I had no idea how he knew I'd jumped ship, and I couldn't believe that I'd been found out so quickly.

"Get up! Come on now." He was waving at me to stand, and I slowly got to my feet. He was older than me and certainly slower. I was sure that if we were out in the open, I'd be able to outrun him. But there, on the back of the bus, he had me cornered. There was no easy escape for me. So I did what he asked and followed him back down the aisle.

A little way down he stopped, turned to me, and pointed

at an empty seat. He wasn't yelling so much now, and I was able to pick out a few words, like "Blacks…" and "whites…" When I sat down he seemed happier and walked back to the front of the bus. It was only as we drove off that I noticed a chain behind me and a sign indicating that the seats at the back of the bus were "Colored Only."

The American South of the early sixties was nothing like the Bay Area or Boston's western suburbs. I wasn't prepared for it, and I didn't know that a white-skinned illegal immigrant like myself had more rights, privileges, and freedoms than the Black American citizens sitting behind me, whose ancestors had been brought here against their will. It wasn't right.

I stayed quiet for the rest of the journey to Jacksonville, Florida. It was late, and many of the rest of my fellow passengers were sleeping, but I was wide awake, braced for whatever was coming next.

At 2:00 a.m. we pulled into the bus depot in Tallahassee. There was an hour to wait until the next bus arrived, and I found a bench near a broken-down fence that I could easily escape through with a clear view of the depot. My body was starting to feel tired from all the tension, but I was as wired and alert as I'd ever been in my life.

I'd been waiting thirty or forty minutes when I heard shouting. This time it wasn't a single person, but two groups each of ten or more young Black men started to yell and scream at each other on the far side of the depot. I watched carefully. I had seen plenty of street shouting battles in Athens, and most of the time the anger evaporated quickly enough.

But this was different. The shouting grew louder, the body language more aggressive. Soon someone pulled out a baseball bat. I saw the glint of a knife. Then everything erupted. They were twenty or thirty feet away from me, but the speed at which things were moving had me worried. I looked down behind me at the broken fence and saw a two-by-four piece of wood, which I quietly placed behind me on the bench. If they came close, I'd have to defend myself.

The fight continued to rage, but luckily the bus pulled in early, and the brawlers moved away. I joined the few people cautiously getting on board, all the time keeping an eye out. Only when the bus pulled out again did I feel like I could breathe freely. I crossed myself several times. I could feel people's eyes on me, but for once I didn't mind. I was just grateful to be relatively safe again.

Most people slept on the three-hour drive to Jacksonville, but not me. I was still too wired to sit still, let alone sleep. I sat and fidgeted with my magazine, wishing the night would pass and eager to be out of the South.

The half-hour stop in Jacksonville passed without incident, and I spent a few precious cents on a burger and coffee. Then it was back onto another bus for a fifteen-hour drive to Richmond, Virginia, followed by a long final leg that would take me all the way to my destination. By that time I was exhausted, too tired even to sleep, let alone talk. But as we pushed north on the final bus, the young woman sitting next to me wanted to talk.

"Where are you going?"

"Philly," I said, trying to rid myself of my Greek accent. I was naturally suspicious of anyone asking me questions, but I didn't want to appear nervous at all.

"Oh, that's nice," she smiled. "I got family there." She carried on telling me all about her different family members, what they did, what they were like. I tried to keep my mouth shut and only speak when I absolutely had to, but this didn't seem to trouble her. She was just a nice, friendly person, and I could feel myself relax in her company. It was good to be reminded of the fact that I had lived happily and without fear in America for many months the last time I was there.

Eventually, after three grueling days on multiple buses, my long journey was finally over. I stepped off the bus in Philly on October 29, said goodbye to my friendly companion, and paused. It was 4:00 a.m., and the sky was ink black and bitterly cold. The other passengers scattered, and there was nobody else around. I was alone. It was time to begin again. I found a taxi to drive me to my uncle's restaurant on Market Street.

Standing outside my uncle's twenty-four-hour restaurant when it was still dark outside, I felt a little nervous. This was the man who sent us all those gifts for so many years—the basketballs, the clothes, even the mule. He left Greece after the First World War and never returned. Even though I had never met him in person, when I was a child, he took on gigantic proportions in my mind, as if he lived like a king in a palace. Standing on the cold street looking at the Market Street Diner, I wondered briefly what I would find inside. Would I be disappointed? Would he?

I needn't have worried. As soon as I saw Uncle Alex, we embraced and both of us started crying. For him, it was emotional to see his sister's son when he hadn't seen her for thirty-five years. For me, it was another opportunity to reconnect with family. After three days of worrying on the buses, and thirty-five days before that when I was at sea and wondering how I would jump ship, it felt good to be a son again, to be embraced by someone I could trust completely. I was no longer on my own.

Uncle Alex introduced me to his wife, Georgia, and showed me around his restaurant. We talked for much of the morning about my parents back in Greece, my uncle and aunt's own experience of living in America, and my plans to return to Boston. My aunt took me shopping for some spare clothes and made up a bed for me at their house. They had no children of their own, and by the end of the day, we felt like a little family of our own.

My experience working for Mr. Contos made me a useful asset to them, and I was happy to help out at their restaurant working in the kitchen, starting the very next day. Despite my getting arrested at the diner before, I felt comfortable in restaurants. I liked the noise of indistinguishable conversations, the smell of good food, and the laughter of satisfied customers as they savored the experience. I was happy doing whatever my uncle and aunt needed me to do, and by the end of the first day, I felt as though I'd never been away.

The restaurant was bigger than Mr. Contos's diner, and the clientele made a lot more noise. They seemed to discuss everything, only at maximum volume.

"You've arrived at an interesting time," Uncle Alex explained when I pointed this out as he, Aunt Georgia, and I drank a coffee together at the end of the evening rush. "They're not usually this loud."

He explained that the country was about to vote. I knew nothing of politics but was interested to learn about American life, so I listened hard as my uncle explained about the different candidates, their parties, and the reasons why opinion in the restaurant was so divided.

"It's this Democrat guy," he said. "No way is he gonna win. America will never vote in a Catholic as a president."

Aunt Georgia disagreed. "He'll win. I saw it in a dream."

Uncle Alex dismissed her with a wave of the hand, but she wasn't deterred. "I saw Franklin Roosevelt dead in his casket, and an image of John Kennedy came out of his stomach."

Uncle Alex laughed along with the few other diners that were still lingering around. Aunt Georgia stuck to her guns and pointed to the front page of a newspaper. "I'm telling you, this Kennedy guy's our next president."

The name sounded familiar. I took a close look at the newspaper.

And there he was: the very man who had secured my release from the Charles Street Jail when I was arrested. I wanted to shout out and tell everyone the story, but thought better of it. I buried it deep inside. I had no right to vote in the election, but I decided then and there that if ever I did become a citizen and had the chance to vote, I would cast my ballot for Mr. John F. Kennedy. I knew from personal experience that he was a good man who could be trusted. In his hands, I was sure that America would prosper.

I also learned that each political party had a logo: a donkey for the Democrats and an elephant for the Republicans. Georgia's brother painted the two animals in front of the white refrigerator fighting each other. I thought it was funny and very interesting. The day after Senator Kennedy won the 1960 election, Georgia's brother painted the donkey kicking the elephant.

A week later I left Philadelphia. It was sad to say goodbye to my Uncle Alex and the restaurant. I spent three happy weeks there, earning enough money to repay Dimitri and making friends among the customers. I listened to them argue about the election and developed my own fascination with American politics—a fascination that would continue to grow and thrive in the decades to come.

I didn't travel alone. Aunt Georgia agreed to travel with me, knowing that I was far less likely to stand out to any suspicious eyes if I was traveling with her, and that if anyone did get curious about my immigration status, she could talk us out of trouble. It was also a way of avoiding my getting confused at Grand Central and jumping onto the wrong train. I was a little nervous at the prospect of making the journey—still slightly on edge from the epic journey from Mobile—and the thought of having my aunt beside me calmed my nerves considerably.

You can thank the Greeks for why Philadelphia is known

as the city of brotherly love. The name is a combination of our words for friend (phileo) and brother (adelphos), and I left the city feeling full of gratitude for the love of my uncle and aunt. Yet, as my aunt and I threaded our way north toward Boston's South Street station, I could feel my sense of anticipation grow. My uncle and aunt worked hard and were dedicated to their local church, but with no children and not too many other interests, they were not as connected to their local community as my friends in Watertown were. I had loved my time in Philly, but heading back to Boston felt as though I was returning home.

I have often thought about the influence of the Greek community here in Boston on my life, especially about the role of the church within it. For me, it all started the day Father Metaxas invited me back to his house after church. It was a simple enough gesture and one that cost him only a few cents and an hour or two of his time on a busy Sunday, but it made a significant impact on me. Father Metaxas did not wait to offer his friendship until I joined the church and started giving my time or money. He did not wait until he figured out what kind of Christian I was—whether I was truly an Orthodox believer or whether I was just there for the routine and the ritual. He did not even wait to work out what I was doing in the Boston area and to determine whether I was an illegal immigrant or not. He just offered me, a stranger, a place at his table.

For so many Greeks all over the world, the Orthodox church and their local Greek community are pillars in their

George E. Danis

# HERE'S MY BEGINNING . . .

My mother in 1920 with her parents.

My parents Stilyanni and Evangelos on their wedding day in 1935.

Family photo in front of our home in 1945. I am next to my father.

Castle behind my childhood home built by the Romans.

When I left Greece at age 18 on my way to Germany to embark on the *Atlantic Sea.*

Serving in the Greek Navy, with the NATO forces.

Life on the ship *Atlantic Sea* traveling around the world for years. I am the second from right, the tallest one.

# STARTING MY NEW LIFE AND FAMILY IN AMERICA

To my first wife Katerina, nicknamed Sookie, a wonderful mother who took care of our four amazing daughters: Stella, Barbara, Marina, and Jennifer. Thank you very much, Sookie!

My lovely daughters home from school for the holidays.

At the age of 2, my grandson Christopher and me working to live from the land.

Navigating from Annapolis, Maryland, to Boston, through a stormy Atlantic Ocean. I'm the one in the middle.

My grandchildren, twins Alexandra and Stephanie (3), William (2) in the middle, Christopher, and my nephew Philip at the twins' birthday party.

# LIFE AND FAMILY IN AMERICA

Me explaining to Christopher (6) where I came from, while visiting my childhood home.

Praying for no rain at my daughter Barbara's wedding in Copper Mountain, Colorado. And it worked!

And we continued dancing Greek!

Showing my daughter Barbara and my grandchildren Theodore (4) and Anna (2) where I grew up.

On my 80th birthday, I am surrounded by my amazing nine grandchildren and my lovely wife Karen.

I am hovering over my two older brothers enjoying dinner at a tavern in Greece.

# LIFE AND FAMILY IN AMERICA

Having a wonderful time with my marvelous wife and grandson Christopher at a gala in West Palm Beach.

GEORGE EVANGELOS DANIS
born Friday July 17, 1937 * Milos, Greece
son of Evangelos & Stilyanni Ntavns
brother to Evangelos, Polychroni,
and Alexandros

* son, brother, uncle, husband, father, papou,
friend, mentor, entrepreneur, restaurateur,
Ellis Island Medal of Honor Recipient,
philanthropist, radio & tv personality,
poliical analyst & philosopher *

My daughters, their spouses, and my grandchildren presented this to me as a gift for my 80th birthday.

Anna Korfmacher
1/20/17

## Land of Hope

    The first time I came here I was extremely nervous,
But I had to go back to Greece to do military service,
Then finally when the time came of age,
I was ready to find a new home and start a new page,
So I said farewell to my family in our petite little shack,
And brought a few belongings in a tiny cloth sack,
Then I boarded a huge crowded boat,
One that I hoped would stay afloat.
    I then was afraid for what if nothing works,
Who knows of in this land what lurks,
Then suddenly I saw her in her marvelous green glory,
She is the reason I am here telling this story,
She is a bright shining beacon of hope,
She made me certain that I could cope,
It was as if someone was reaching out a hand,
It was then I realized it was this devoted, fond land.
    Now in this land I have a story to tell,
With my children and grandchildren my life is going well,
I have a successful business I made out of nothing,
This is proof that when you think there is hate, you can find loving,
To every immigrant who is alone and afraid,
Look at every immigrant here, see what we have made,
To everyone that thinks that they cannot cope,
Come here and you will be secure in this land of hope.

I am grateful to my granddaughter Anna, at the age of 13, for this brilliant poem that encouraged me to write my story.

# MY POLITICAL INVOLVEMENT

Here I am having a political discussion with former president of the Soviet Union, Mikhail Gorbachev.

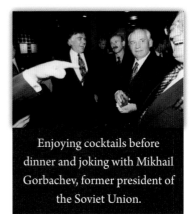

Enjoying cocktails before dinner and joking with Mikhail Gorbachev, former president of the Soviet Union.

Presenting an award to my friend George Behrakis in Washington, DC.

Senator John Kerry and I celebrating his election to the Senate.

Receiving a business award from Gov. Mike Dukakis.

Gov. Dukakis, Senator Paul Sarbanes, and I hosting a breakfast for the Precinct Captains in Iowa the week of the caucus.

Hosting a fundraising event for Congressman Joe Kennedy at the Ship Restaurant.

# MY POLITICAL INVOLVEMENT

I am cracking the Easter egg with presidential candidate and Gov. Michael Dukakis for good luck.

Accompanying presidential candidate Gov. Dukakis to Iowa.

Accompanying Senator Edward Kennedy to my daugher Marina's school for Constitution Week.

Here I am attending a fundraiser with my friend George for then-Senator Joe Biden in 2008.

Meeting Senator Tsongas and strategizing his candidacy for the 1992 Democratic nomination for the presidency.

My frequent appearance on the Grecian Echoes Radio Program.

I was invited to be a commentator on the GREEK BOSTON television program on the eve of the Presidential election on November 7, 2016.

# MY BUSINESS ENDEAVORS

At the age of 21, with a bow tie, me, on the left, hosting a dinner for my Sales Team, strategizing my first business endeavor selling cloth door-to-door in Greece.

Playing volleyball with my business associates.

Receiving an award from *USA Today*.

CEO GEORGE DANIS receives award from *USA Today* President and Publisher Thomas Curley on behalf of Plastic Molding Manufacturing.

## Plastic Molding Manufacturing receives national award

Receiving an award from AT&T.

Operating and developing the iconic Ship Restaurant and Christmas Tree Shop on Route 1 in Lynnfield, Massachusetts.

The Ship restaurant and Christmas Tree Shop in Lynnfield.

# MY SPIRITUAL LEADERS

Here I am hosting Ecumenical Patriarch Demetrios on his visit to Boston in 1990.

Attending a meeting with my spiritual leader Archbishop Iakovos of the Americas.

I was receiving an award from my spiritual leader Metropolitan Methodios and my mentor Father Metaxas on my right.

Enjoying dinner with, from the left, Former Queen Anna Maria of Greece, Metropolitan Methodios, my lovely wife Karen, and me, half-hidden on the right.

lives. Religion, culture, and family cannot be separated, and for many of us, so much of our life flows in and out of the church and the community. We are strengthened by our connection to both, and I believe that a good part of the success of the Greek diaspora in the fields of education and business is due to our strong roots of faith and community.

Faith has always been important to me, and I try to let God guide my path. In all my years I have never questioned the religion I was brought up in. I have never seen religion as a means to secure my eternal salvation nor have I ever seen it as a means of improving my social status. The church is like my family: it's something I support because we are deeply connected. I don't give because I expect to receive something in return. I give because generosity has been shown to me so many times by so many people that I can't think of a better way to live my life than to imitate those people as best I can.

Arriving back in Boston, I quickly felt the warm embrace of the community. Mr. and Mrs. Contos invited me to eat with them and even offered me a room in their beautiful home, rent free, while I got myself on my feet. I gladly accepted their generous offer as well as the invitation to return to work at the diner.

Mr. Contos and I both felt that my previous position of short-order cook wasn't suitable anymore. It wasn't wise for me to be so visible in the restaurant, and so I was given a job working down in the basement kitchen, helping Ed the baker, working from midnight until first light. It was a job that had some serious upsides.

Ed was a genius with desserts. In all my life both before and since, I've never tasted an éclair or a banana cream pie that was even remotely as good as his. He had a way of combining delicate flavors and unbelievable textures that made it impossible for you to stop at just one. Working in the restaurant before I was deported, I'd seen women close their eyes in pleasure and grown men swear with joy as they bit into one of Ed's creations. And now that I was back and assigned to him, I had the best job in the whole diner. Every time I went to the refrigerator when Ed was out of the kitchen, I would grab an éclair, cram it into my mouth, and swallow it as fast as I could.

Mr. Contos's help didn't stop at employment and accommodations, either. He was determined to help me find a permanent, viable solution to my immigration problem. In other words, a wife with citizenship.

One evening, not too long after I arrived in Boston, a prominent couple within the local community was invited to dinner. They came alone, leaving their daughter at home, as was the custom in many Greek communities. The first meeting was the opportunity for the girl's parents to check me out for themselves, to see whether I matched up to whatever description Mr. or Mrs. Contos had given of me. I must have passed because soon after I was out on a date with their daughter, Toula.

Toula picked me up in an old green-and-white Chevrolet, and we spent the evening going to dinner and the movies. She spoke Greek while I spoke English, and she was great—good company and easy to be around—but there was no real romantic connection. One date was enough for both of us to know that there was no future for us.

Mrs. Contos was not deterred. She introduced me to a niece of hers named Marsha. We went out on several dates around the holiday period, and I quickly learned that Marsha was unlike any of the other Greek women I'd met before, either back home or in the United States. Marsha was brought up within the Greek community, but she had a decidedly American way of looking at the world. She was outspoken, rarely seeming to feel the need to hold back her opinions. She was outgoing, too, dating more than one man at a time. She knew what she wanted, and she didn't see why anything as old and outdated as social convention should prevent her from getting it. It was 1960, and she was ahead of her time.

I, on the other hand, was behind, with a worldview that was still shaped by my upbringing in rural Greece. With differences like these, Marsha and I were never going to be able to form any kind of lasting relationship, but we did become good friends.

It wasn't until almost Christmas that I finally met someone who seemed right for me. I'd been invited to a Christmas party hosted by George, one of the Contos's three sons, at his home in Belmont. I wasn't looking for a wife that night, but when I was introduced to Katherine Banakos, I was intrigued—here was a woman who was both Greek and American, someone who appeared to belong fully to both worlds. We spent much of the evening talking to each other and, by the end of it, agreed to go out on a date together.

Something about Marsha must have rubbed off on me because I decided to be totally honest with Kathy from the very start. I told her on our first date that, even though marriage would fix my immigration problem, I wanted more than that.

"I want to find the person I can spend the rest of my life with," I said, trying to use my best English but struggling with a few of the words. "It's really important to me that you understand this."

It was a strong statement to make back in the early sixties, particularly between two people who were brought up within the Greek community. Among my people, nobody frowned on the idea of marriage as a practical solution to the problems of being single, and my parents both entered their relationship with a clear idea of the benefits their union would bring, especially to my mother. But talking about love and being committed in an honest, open discussion at the start was definitely unusual. Kathy thought hard about my words. She didn't flinch or withdraw but simply nodded and smiled.

A week after our first date—during which Kathy invited me to join her babysitting her nieces, and it was clear that something special was happening between us—the subject of marriage came up again. We were eating in a Chinese restaurant, and I was convinced that Kathy was the right one for me. As far as I could tell, there were only two main hurdles to our getting married.

The first was money for an engagement ring, which was nothing new for me. I'd always had ideas beyond my budget and always found a way of either earning or borrowing and paying back the money I needed. The second hurdle was Chinese food, which Kathy liked but I had never tried. As we sat and talked about the future life we might build together, I struggled with the range of new tastes and smells. It took all my strength to fight back the urge to push all the food away from me. But Kathy was happy—with the food, the company, and the concept of spending life together and raising a family.

With that agreed, it was time to make plans. I had no money saved, and having finally moved out of the Contos's spare bedroom, my wages from the diner were almost all taken up with rent. The Contos family came to the rescue yet again. Mr. and Mrs. George Contos loaned me $750 for a ring—a colossal amount in those days, especially for someone with as little earning potential as mine—and helped organize a quick civil wedding with a justice of the peace. It was a big ring, but a small ceremony: just Kathy and me, her parents, her sister Jenny, Mr. and Mrs. Contos, and the justice of the peace, a Greek man called Monty Basbas. I met him years later, and he was elected mayor of Newton before becoming a federal judge. We became very good friends and talked about the marriage he performed for us.

We had moved fast. We were married at the end of December 1960, less than two months after I had jumped ship in Mobile and sat nervously on the bus, desperately hoping that nobody would notice me. Kathy and I had known each other for only fourteen days, but I was sure that we were right for each other and could look forward to a long, happy future together raising a family.

But not quite yet. Now that I was married, I had taken a big step toward being allowed to remain in America legally, but officially I was still an illegal alien. In order to be granted residency and finally be able to step out from the shadows, I would need to do one more thing: I had to go back home to Greece and secure official permission to return to the United States.

## CHAPTER EIGHT
# THE WAY BACK IS THE WAY FORWARD

I WOKE UP READY FOR CHANGE on the day that the thirty-fifth president of the United States of America was being sworn into office. I didn't join the crowds to witness the ceremony and celebrate the arrival of John F. Kennedy into the White House, but it was impossible to avoid the TV screens and front pages of newspapers. JFK was everywhere you looked, smiling, waving, urging us to ask not what our country could do for us but what we could do for our country. It was the dawn of a new era, a time of possibility and progress. It spoke deep to my soul. But I wasn't sticking around to listen.

On January 20, 1961, I was once again making my way back to Greece. I landed a job as a deckhand on board an Italian cruise ship heading to Naples. It took two-and-a-half weeks to reach the port, then a few more days by train to Brindisi to make my way back toward Patras and Athens, but soon enough I was back in my homeland, embracing Polychronis and losing myself in the familiar chaos and warmth of Greek life. I was happy to see my family again, but Athens no longer felt like home. It felt like the place I needed to visit in order to leave again and return to the new home I had chosen.

The list of things I had to attend to in Greece was short but daunting. I needed a visa from the American embassy and a passport from the Greek authorities. Today, those tasks would require a lot of online form filling, but back in 1961 the challenge was finding someone within each office who would be prepared to lend a hand and hurry your application along.

The evening I arrived in Athens, I told Polychronis about my needing a passport and a visa and how I hoped to get them both and be back home to my wife sometime around Easter. "As soon as I get back, we can have our Orthodox wedding ceremony. After that we can finally live as man and wife and make a start on our family."

He frowned.

"What?" I asked.

"Two years," he said. "That's how long it will take you to get a passport and visa."

By now Polychronis was working for Greece's equivalent of the CIA, and I trusted his opinion more than anyone else's. He knew the way the state worked and had firsthand experience of the bureaucracy and inefficiency that plagued the country's systems. But I refused to believe that I would have to wait so long. I *couldn't* wait that long. The thought of being away from Kathy for so long was just too terrible to even consider. So I did what any younger brother would do when given unpleasant advice from their older brother, and I ignored it completely.

The next morning I went straight to the American embassy, giving them all the paperwork that I could prepare and more from the federal authorities in Boston. I was keen to start the process of applying for my visa. They were polite and efficient, and I felt sure that I would soon be able to prove my brother wrong.

The Greek foreign affairs office was a different story altogether. These were the days when all the young Greeks were emigrating all over the world, and all of them wanted a passport. The line of people waiting to be seen was vast, snaking out of the office and down the stairs. It took me hours to reach the front and ask for an application form, and when I did I was told to return with it in a few weeks when the demand for passports had decreased a little.

It was late in the evening by the time I returned to Polychronis's house. I knew he was right about how long it would take, but I didn't like it. And I refused to accept it. I was determined to find a way forward. I did not want to be stuck thousands of miles away from Kathy, blocked by a bunch of bureaucrats from starting the new life in Boston that I was desperate to begin.

Being back in Athens did have some advantages, like being able to travel back to the island often to see my parents. I'd last seen them the previous summer, and little had changed in their lives, but there was a lot to catch up on. They were eager to hear about Kathy and her family. It concerned them that they knew nothing of the woman their son had married, but they trusted all four of us boys to do the right thing.

What concerned all of us more was the fact that I had no idea when I might return to America. Marrying Kathy and deciding to start a family together meant that a significant period in my life was coming to an end. America really would be my home from now on, and as soon as I received my passport and visa, there would be no risk of me being deported back to Greece. I would try to visit my parents as often as I could, but I had no idea when that would be.

A few weeks after my failed attempt to apply for a passport, my other brothers Evangelos and Alexandros were in town, and the four of us went out for lunch together at a restaurant not far from the passport office. As we sat around a table filled with stuffed vegetables, moussaka, and lamb baked with garlic and rosemary, the subject of my task came up in conversation. Like typical brothers, they teased me a little about my earlier optimism and were eager to share stories of other people they knew who had endured years-long waits for their passports.

"Two years for a passport would be quick," added Evangelos, which set the other two nodding.

"Well," I said as I stood up, straightened my tie, and put my suit jacket on, "I'm not so sure. I think I'll go check."

"I wouldn't bother," said Polychronis.

I wasn't listening. I was already walking away from the table and heading back to the passport office.

The line of people was even longer this time, but I had a plan. I picked up my pace as I entered the building and strode up the stairs two at a time, skipping the line entirely.

As I reached the desks where the clerks sat, a space opened up, and I jumped right in.

"I need your help," I said to the young man. "I just came back from America. I got married out there, and my wife is home alone without her new husband." The clerk returned my smile. "She's pregnant, too," I lied. "So please, can you help me? I can't wait years for a passport. I've got my application here. It's got everything that you could possibly need in it."

I slid the paper forms over the desk, careful that only the clerk could see the five hundred drachmas I had placed between the pages. I noticed his eyes widen just a little when he saw the money. Fifteen dollars was a lot of money in those days, especially to a Greek man working in the passport office.

"Let me see," he said, carefully gathering up my application and the gift within and disappearing through a door in the back.

I settled down and prepared to wait, not knowing how long he would be and hoping that my bold move would pay off. I had seen enough of the world by then to know that money could unlock plenty of doors, and I was confident that this guy was willing to help. But after five minutes of waiting, a first twinge of doubt flashed through me. What if he had taken offense? What if I'd been wrong?

I didn't have to wonder for long. A few minutes later he was back, handing me my brand new Greek passport.

My brothers were still sitting at the table when I got back to the restaurant.

"You were quick," said Polychronis. "Did you even get to talk to anyone?"

I said nothing but pulled my passport out and let them pass it around. They were amazed and were desperate to know how I'd managed it.

"It was easy," I said. "I told them I had three brothers waiting outside who would be very upset if I didn't get what I wanted." They started to laugh, just as happy as I was.

Now that I had my Greek passport, I returned to the American embassy first thing the next morning. I was wearing the same suit and tie, though I decided against offering a bribe. Instead, I made up my mind to be likable, presentable, and honest. So I handed in my application with the passport, told my story about being married—though not the lie about Kathy being pregnant—and hoped that it would work.

"Come back again next week," said the unmoved clerk, whose face was expressionless and cold, as if he were one year into a lifetime prison sentence.

"Okay…," I said, looking down at the nameplate on the desk in front of me, "…Neil. I will come back. Tomorrow."

Neil frowned and called the next person forward.

I was back at Neil's desk the next morning, asking for an update on my application. There was none, so I left him, saying, "See you tomorrow."

There was no change the next day, either. Neil was still unable to give me any kind of update on when my visa application would be considered, and his face remained a stony mask.

I went every day that week and was there again on Monday morning when the embassy opened after the weekend.

Neil wasn't quite so stern with me that morning. He almost managed a smile and offered me a bit of friendly advice.

"You know that you don't have to visit every day, don't you?"

"I know that. But I am happy to do it. This way you will not forget me."

He smiled a little, then told me the same thing he had said every day. "There's still no news on your application. Come back in a few weeks."

Tuesday's and Wednesday's visits went exactly the same way. On Thursday, however, Neil told me that he was not going to be working the next day. "So there really isn't any point in you coming in then, is there?"

I nodded and started to make my plan.

The next day I strolled in and waited to be seen. Just as he'd said, there was no sign of Neil, and I waited to speak to one of his colleagues.

"Hello…Arthur," I said, checking the name on the desk when it was my turn to be seen. "Neil told me to come in and collect my visa."

"Neil's not in today."

"I know that, but he told me to come and ask someone else here. My name is George Danis."

Arthur looked at me a while, then shrugged and left his desk. I waited a little longer than I had to wait for my passport, but eventually my plan paid off, and Arthur returned with a fully approved visa allowing me to travel to the United States of America freely and legally.

I played it cool, not wanting to arouse suspicion. I thanked Arthur, left the embassy, and headed straight for the island.

It was hard to say goodbye to my parents. I wanted to savor every last moment with them, but there was a choking feeling inside that would not be ignored. I had no idea if that might be the last time I would see either of them, and the thought was like poison.

Later, I found out that my parents struggled, too. My mother did no housework for a week, which is the traditional way a grieving mother mourns the death of a child. For years she prayed silently in front of photographs of me.

But I had to go. My life was no longer among the hills and goat tracks of Mili, the warm skies of Karystos, or even in the chaos and excitement of Athens. My future was in America, just as I had hoped it would be when I first left on the *Atlantic Sea* all those years before.

In the last days of March, 1961, just two months after I said goodbye to Kathy in Boston, I began my journey back to America. Now that I was a married man with official permission to enter the United States through the front door, there was no time for slow sea journeys back across the Atlantic or meandering trips that took me halfway around the world while I earned a little money on the side. I was in a rush to get back and be reunited with my wife.

I flew Sabena Airlines, Athens to Brussels, Belgium, my first ever time in an airplane. Then it was a direct flight to New York City's Idlewild Airport, now known as JFK. I hopped on another flight with American Airlines up to Boston and stepped into the arrivals hall. I was home. I was legal. I was ready to get married in a church with Father Metaxas presiding, ready to start this new and wonderful life I'd been looking forward to for so long.

The only problem was there was no sign at all of Kathy. Despite the fact that I'd told her about my flights, she didn't turn up. I waited a while, wondering if maybe she'd just gotten confused about the timings. But I was feeling tired from the traveling, my head feeling heavy and my limbs starting to ache. I soon started to feel worried about her not being there. I'd been away for two months. Had she forgotten about me already? What happened to those conversations about ours being a proper marriage, not just one of convenience?

It was late, so I took a taxi to Mr. Contos's house. I called Kathy at her job the next morning, feeling a whole lot better from the whole night's sleep. We figured out what happened and how she'd gotten confused about the flight times. Soon everything was okay between us again, and we were able to get on with the task at hand: planning our wedding.

On our wedding day—June 5, 1961—I walked alone from my room nearby to the church and looked around at the assembled guests. It was a bittersweet feeling. I was so happy to be able to finally get married in a church and happy, too, that I found a good woman with whom I could start a family. Kathy's family and friends were all there, about sixty people in all. I had nothing like so many people. Mr. and

Mrs. Contos were there and so were my mother's cousin Alex, and Katherine, who I stayed with when I first came to Boston. But Uncle Alex and Aunt Georgia weren't able to make it. Father Metaxas was there, just as I always knew he would be, but I felt the absence of so many people. My brothers, my parents, my other relatives from Greece—none of them were able to fly out to join us and neither were any of my friends.

This was it. This was what I had been hoping and planning for over the previous years. I was starting the biggest challenge of my life, and I had never felt quite so alone.

My mind went back to when I said goodbye to my parents in Mili. I felt the same wrenching sensation again, felt the true cost of what it means to be an immigrant: that in order to leave your homeland and start afresh somewhere new, you must bury a part of yourself.

If you want to build a new life, you must be prepared to fight for it with every breath in your body. And the challenge was great. Like most young people at that time, I decided to leave Greece. It was different this time because I knew that I was making a new life for myself away from my homeland. To leave my family, the people I relied on for support, advice, and help in every step of my life, was painful. I had community and friends in the United States, but it wasn't the same.

At times I felt as if no one was around for me. At times I felt as if I were alone.

# PART
# TWO

# CHAPTER NINE
# A QUESTION OF DESIRE

SOCRATES AND PLATO were walking one day, when young Plato asked a question.

"How do I become successful?"

Socrates thought a while and paused. They were standing near a water trough, and the older man leaned over the water, beckoning Plato to do the same. When Plato's head was over the water, Socrates grabbed him by the back of the neck and forced his head down. Plato twisted and thrashed, trying to release himself from the old man's grip, but it was no use. Socrates was old, but he was strong. The younger man's life was in his hands.

When Socrates thought that Plato was on the verge of losing consciousness, he pulled him out and watched him gasping for air, a mix of fear and anger in his eyes.

"Why?" Plato coughed.

"You want success?" Socrates smiled. "You must learn to be as desperate for it as you were for air just now. Only when you are prepared to fight for success as a matter of life or death will you find it."

I doubt the story is strictly accurate, but it contains a pearl of human wisdom that is profoundly true: if we want to achieve anything of real worth in life, we must be prepared to give everything we have in its pursuit. We must be resilient and resourceful, endure all kinds of setbacks and disappointments, and overcome all manner of obstacles. We must be prepared to adopt an attitude that is relentless in its positivity while at the same time being reflective and self-critical when necessary. We will fall down and fail again and again and again, but what matters more than the mistakes we make are the lessons we learn from them. We must be prepared to fight—not necessarily against others but against our own fear and self-doubt.

---

I was like the young Plato during the early years of my new life in America. I was determined to build a life for Kathy and the family we anticipated would soon follow, and I was willing to work harder than I had ever worked in my life before. But there was one difference between my situation and the Plato story: I was not focused on success. I wanted enough money to live on, but money was never my ultimate goal. I was an engineer at heart and a lifelong addict to the pursuit of my own curiosity. All I really wanted was to build for myself the kind of work life that would allow me to thrive. If I did have any idea of what success would look like, it was owning my own restaurant like Mr. Contos or having enough money to be able to invite a house full of guests over and feed them steak and beer, just as Vasillis Novas did when we met him in Oakland.

I pushed myself hard with whatever I did. I worked nights in a diner when Kathy and I were first married, then found a job in another diner that would let me work during the day. This allowed Kathy and me to spend more time together at our home in Newton on California Street and also meant that I could study engineering at a school nearby and take English classes too. When the diner owners offered me a job running their other restaurant in Bedford, Massachusetts, I was happy to accept. It meant starting work at 5:00 a.m., but the promotion from short-order cook to manager was huge for me. I was moving forward in my life.

The diner in Bedford was about ten miles away from the home we rented, and even on the drive there and back, I was looking for opportunities to pursue my curiosity. When I saw an empty restaurant that was for rent, I pulled over, and went exploring. I found out that the place was fully equipped with everything you would need to start it up again—all the kitchen appliances, tables, chairs, and dining essentials. Even better was the fact that the owners were willing to waive the first three or four months' rent. All I would need was enough money to buy the first food order.

By the time I got home, I was excited and ready to sign the lease papers. But Kathy had a simple question for me that made me stop and think.

"Do you have the money to cover that first food order and pay the wait staff?"

I paused. It didn't take long to add up all the money I had in savings, and the total was barely enough to fill our own pantry, let alone stock an entire restaurant with enough food to generate a week's pay to cover the purchase of food and supplies for next week. So it didn't take long for me to accept the fact that I was too cash poor to take on that particular business opportunity.

Once I had closed off that possibility in my mind, I was able to see clearly: I knew a little about working in restaurants but only because working in restaurants was the only option open to me when I first lived in the United States. I liked being a short-order cook, but I had never chosen to be one. My curiosity never really turned in that direction, apart from the occasional time as a child when I helped my mother prepare food. I found restaurants interesting, and it was easy enough to work in one, but I was not yet ready to devote all of my energies to making a success of my own diner. I wanted more, to allow my curiosity to take charge and to pursue the kind of work that captured my imagination since I was a young child.

Back in the sixties there was no unemployment check to collect, no big government support that would allow people to remain out of work, indefinitely collecting benefits. Instead, government assistance amounted to an unemployment office where you could go to search for a job. If you were unemployed, you got nothing, so anyone who wanted to change careers as I did had to be prepared to fight like Plato struggling for air.

George E. Danis

I decided that I wanted to work in engineering and made regular visits to the unemployment office to try and land myself a job. It took time and persistence, but eventually I was told about an opening at a metal fabrication factory nearby. I went for an interview, was given the job, and spent the next few days feeling increasingly excited about the opportunity to learn how to make different cabinets and housing for the electronics industry.

The next day I gave my notice to the restaurant owner, and a week later I finished working there.

I showed up for work on my first day, eager to impress. I lasted two hours.

I'd not seen the factory floor when I was interviewed, and I was shocked to discover just how bad the levels of air pollution were down there among the machines. There was no ventilation, no protection, and the combination of smoke and chemicals burned the back of my throat. I was all for being curious and determined and digging in for the fight, but not if it meant vaporizing my lungs in the process.

I went back to the unemployment office and persuaded them to help me find another job. I next landed a position at a local engineering company, McNab's, where I was given the task of chemical washing the aluminum. I showed up on my first day and again found that I was in line for smoky, unpleasant work, but my boss, Charlie, was a good guy, and I figured that if I went back and complained again, I'd run out of luck with the unemployment office. So I dug in, worked hard and fast, and trusted that something good would come of it.

By lunchtime I washed all the aluminum parts I had been given and called Charlie over to show him.

He looked at me weirdly. "You did what?"

My English was still poor, and I was a little worried that I had not understood his original instruction. "I finished washing them. Did I do something wrong?"

"No." He smiled, checking over my work. "The last two guys would take a whole day to do all this."

From then on I was set. I continued working as hard and fast as possible, and within weeks Charlie rewarded my efforts—and my constant curiosity about the rest of the factory's equipment—by moving me on to better tasks. I was soon making tools and discovering that my instincts about engineering were right: it was the career for me.

Five months after I had started working there, Charlie took me aside one day and told me he had bad news. "We just lost a big contract," he explained, "and I've got to lay you off. But I already found you another job on the other side of town. Pay's 10 percent better, too."

It turned out that Charlie landed me a great job, and the increase to $2.25 per hour was very welcome. After a few months I was able to take over part of the factory while my supervisor was on vacation for a week. And so began a period of my life when I moved from job to job, each one better than the last. In two years I moved again, eventually taking on the job of running the night shift at Honeywell. Each time I took on more responsibilities, earned more money, and learned more about the business of manufacturing. I had a clear goal in mind: to one day start my own manufacturing business. I wanted to be my boss, to do things my way. From my own father to Mr. Contos, I had seen plenty of men do likewise, and I had no reason to doubt that I would succeed.

I needed cash if I was ever going to have any hope of establishing my own company. I made a careful study of the type of machinery required and the price tag for the minimum amount of equipment was easily five figures—a lot more than the amount required to stock a restaurant. I still had barely any savings and needed a way of getting hold of some cash quick.

The answer came to me on the drive home from work. Just like with the restaurant, I saw another property listed for sale, only this time it was an old two-story house on a good lot in Wayland, Massachusetts, near a local bank. It was a wreck, but in my mind it had potential. Best of all, it was cheap: $15,000 with 10 percent down. But even that was a lot of money for me. I had just $900 in my bank account, so I was $600 shy of the deposit. Without that, my plans to flip the property were going nowhere.

This was 1964 and life was already full. Our first daughter, Stella—whom we named after my mother—was approaching her second birthday. She had already brought a lot of joy into our lives, and Stella was part of the reason I was so excited to start my own business in the first place. I wanted to spend more time around my family, not less. If I could create a business that would run without me, I would be free to spend my time as I wished.

Wishing wasn't going to make that $600 shortfall disappear, however, so after thinking hard about possible alternative solutions for a day or two—and coming up with nothing—I was ready to abandon the whole idea. But then a friend of Kathy's came to visit and see Stella. I was telling her about the house, and she offered to loan me the $600. I accepted, knowing that I would pay her back.

A short while later, I was a house owner.

The house was a near-total wreck. Every part of the heating and plumbing system needed replacing, and every room needed decorating, painting, and more. There was no way I could afford to pay someone to do it for me, and I had no previous experience of ever doing any of that kind of work myself. So, on my way to and from work at Honeywell, I became a regular visitor to the local plumbing supply company in Waltham. I'd tell them about my latest challenge—bending pipe or replacing a bathroom set—and they would give me a crash course on whatever I needed to do, right there in the store. Yet again I was struck by the kindness of strangers. It was like being back in the village, supported by a community of benevolent, generous, hardworking people who were willing to do what they could to support me.

It took me months of working every evening and weekend, but eventually I finished the house. I rented it out temporarily and was soon making a good profit each month. I paid back the $600 loan and listed it for sale at $25,000. Trouble was, nobody was interested. The realtor tried to persuade me to drop the price, but between my stubbornness, my confidence, and my need for liquidating as much cash as possible, I refused to listen.

The house went unsold for three years. Nobody was even the slightest bit interested, and I was starting to wonder whether the whole thing was a mistake. And then the bank across the street had a break in. I saw my opportunity.

In those days a lot of banks were converting to drive-throughs to improve their customer service and security. The plot that the branch near me was located on wasn't suitable, but my house was perfect. So I made contact with the head office, explained that I had heard about their recent break in, and offered to sell my house as a tear down. They liked the idea, but when they measured the plot, it wasn't big enough for them. I was back where I started.

My next step was to visit the church next door, thinking they might be interested in purchasing. Their response was clear— "We only accept gifts"—so I moved on, determined to find a buyer.

I was reading the local newspaper one day when I saw an article about a proposal to turn part of a local playground into a car park despite the town's lack of facilities for young children. There was a vote scheduled, and I decided to lend my support to the campaign to keep the playground as it was. The proposal was denied, and so the next day I had my attorney—a Greek guy, Charlie Johnson, who had changed his surname from Yianakopoulos—contact the city council and suggest they buy my house instead and turn it into a parking lot.

They were interested. I opened with $27,000, and we agreed on $26,000. After everything I'd spent, I walked away with $10,000.

I was finally ready to put my plan into action.

I had moved jobs a few times by that point, graduating from machine operator to full-scale engineer production manager. Family life had changed, too: in 1966 Kathy and I welcomed our second daughter, Barbara. I was still studying at evening school, and financially we were living hand to mouth. Life was full, with little margin for error. I was Plato beneath the water, desperate to make things work.

I was working every hour possible, but that didn't mean I was blind to the world around me. Almost a decade had passed since I first arrived in Boston, and already things were changing. The computer age was upon us, and local companies like Honeywell, AT&T, and Data General were some of the biggest names in the industry. They were desperate for companies that could supply the metal cabinets that would house their computers—computers that would fill an entire room. The market was growing exponentially, and I wanted to grab a slice of it.

I had a clear idea what machines I would need and set about trying to find them. My $10,000 felt like a fortune, but it was barely enough to buy one or two brand-new machines. I needed about a dozen, so my only option was to find used machines. Even then, I'd need them to be real bargains.

It took months of looking in the newspaper before I found my first machines—a metal cutting machine and a press brake forming the metal. A rigger I knew from my previous jobs agreed to move them and even offered to store them in his warehouse until I could rent a plant. On and on it went, with me buying more and more machines, each one adding to my growing pile that was taking up space in my rigger's warehouse.

Eventually, I had everything I needed. I spent part of the money I had made on the house sale and needed a building. I saw one place that was for rent, called the number, and someone by the name John answered it. I went to visit John at his office—Guaranty-First Trust, where he was president.

He listened while I explained my plan. I was expecting some kind of negotiation, but what he said surprised me completely.

"Bring your machines," he said. "Once you start making money, you can start paying me."

It was a key moment in my business life, a point at which I was able to make a giant leap forward and establish myself. But there was something else significant about it as well: the lesson that I learned about asking for help. If you are positive, honest, appreciative, and humble, people will be much more inclined to help you than if you try to hide the truth and sell them an inauthentic version of yourself.

Be yourself. Anything else is cheating.

After that great conversation with John, the bank manager, I prepared myself for an awkward conversation with my current boss. Fred was a good man who had always treated me well. I didn't like letting him down, but I was determined to approach the conversation with the same attitude I'd had with John. I didn't want to lie or try to hide the truth. I wanted to be honest and thankful for all he had done for me. How he would respond was out of my control.

I stood in the office at the start of my shift and told Fred that I was handing in my notice.

His response was an immediate: "Why?"

It was a reasonable question. He was paying me $20,000 a year and giving me use of a car—a top wage for any engineer/plant manager at the time. I took a breath and gave him my answer.

"I want to start my own company."

"Doing what?"

Another breath. "Metal fabrication."

If Fred was upset at the news that I was going to be a direct competitor, he didn't show it. He just thought for a while. The room felt small.

"I'll give you a bonus. And shares in the company. Would that make you change your mind?"

"That's kind of you, Fred, thank you. But I really want to be my own boss."

"I can understand that. So let me ask you this, George: Can I invest in your company?"

My head was starting to swim. This was going nothing like how I expected, and the prospect of extra investment was tempting. I had my machinery and my plant but not the cash with which to pay for anything like staff, materials, or utilities. An investor could make the difference between success and failure. And yet something told me that I needed to find a way to decline. It was another Plato moment, a time when I knew I had to fight with everything I had to achieve the goal I set my targets on.

"Fred, that is so kind of you," I said. "But you are busy here. You don't have time to be taking on a partnership in another company. And I have to be honest with you and say that it really matters to me that I take this opportunity to become my own boss. If I have a partner, I'll only be half a boss."

"Boy!" Fred laughed. "You want everything, don't you?"

I got up to leave and start my shift. Then I paused. "You know, if you really want to help me, Fred, you can give me some work. Any jobs that are too small for you, I'll take them on. How does that sound?"

Fred agreed and supplied me with plenty of work that he didn't want or could not do.

---

I started DAMCO—Danis Manufacturing Company—on April 1, 1968. I had no one else working with me, just a floor filled with empty machines. I spent my days traveling around the area, visiting the electronics companies, and looking for work. In the afternoons and evenings, I did the work that Fred was giving me. Gradually, as I started getting my own work, I had to work late into the night to finish it.

One day I called up an old contact who I knew was always looking for good manufacturers. I told him that I wanted him to give me the opportunity to take on any work he had. After he sent me a blueprint for a job and I came in with a price I knew was just below what Fred and any other company would charge, I got the job. It was going to pay $4,000, and I was delighted. But only briefly.

The job required aluminum material. I knew all the best suppliers in the area, and I knew that there was almost no chance of any of them supplying me the metal on account. I would have to pay for it up front, which was impossible. DAMCO was so young, I didn't even have a checkbook. So I dialed the supplier that I had the best relationship with, told him that I had just started DAMCO, and explained that I needed his help. I didn't try to lie or cover up the truth in any way. I just told him my story, plain and simple, and invited him to come down to the plant to see everything for himself. Within the hour the salesperson, Roger Thorley, visited me. After talking with him for a while, Roger smiled.

It worked. He agreed to set up and open an account. Finally, I was in business.

I was both financially strapped and busy with my startup business. Adding to my stress was a letter I received from my brother Polychronis informing me our mother wasn't doing well. They wanted to visit us, to meet Kathy and their granddaughters, Stella and Barbara.

I hadn't seen my parents in over eight years, and I was missing them greatly. I asked my brother to make the arrangements and put them on a flight to New York. In those days you could wait outside the plane, and as my mother and father shuffled off the Olympic Airways flight from Athens, I felt a shock of sadness run through me. Both of them had changed so much in those eight years. They looked old.

The four-hour drive to Boston in my Chevy Impala was full of conversation. There was all the news from Mili to catch up on, and I told them about our family and my life here in the United States. By the time we arrived home, the sadness had eased just a little.

They spent six months with us, and it was a wonderful time. They met Kathy, Stella, and Barbara for the first time, and the young girls loved spending time with their grand-parents. It wasn't the easiest time for me, as it was early on in the life of the business and money was very tight, but we managed well. I took them to Philadelphia to visit my mother's sister-in-law, Georgia—the widow of my mother's deceased brother, Alex. It was a bittersweet time for my parents, my mother especially, who had never seen her brother since he left Greece. But those were the sacrifices that my parents' generation—and the generations before—made. They left everything and traveled to America in the hope of future success for their children.

When their visas were close to expiring, it was time to make arrangements for their return. My brother bought them one-way tickets, so it was up to me to pay the $750 for their return flights. The trouble was, $750 was a lot of money back then, and I didn't have nearly that much saved. My business banker, Charlie Baker, came though, loaning me the entire amount.

We visited New York before their departure, taking in different sites like the Empire State Building, which left them mesmerized. In one of the restaurants in particular, they wanted to order a steak. I forgot to ask the waiter to serve it well done, the way most Greeks eat their meat, so they brought it medium rare. When my mother cut the steak and saw that it was bloody, she cried out, "My boy, this is ready to walk!"

---

Back to manufacturing, the jobs were coming, but saving enough money to grow was another thing. That one job snowballed into dozens. My good friends Jim and Harvey from Data General contracted me, asking me to produce models for the first minicomputers they designed to go to the San Francisco computer show. The models were a huge success, and soon I had more work than I, Paul (my first helper), or the three part-timers could handle—even though we were running the machines through the weekends.

My dreams of expansion were coming true.

Those dreams, just like the whole plan for my business, were not particularly complicated. I had not studied business theory, and I had not spent years and years developing, refining, and revising a business plan. I simply took notice of the world around me, picked up some tips from the best leaders I worked with, and dug deep into the lessons that my parents and community instilled in me as a boy. My business model was as simple as this: I would use all of my energy and intellect to deliver the best products possible, paying the best wages in the market, to the best staff I could find.

I needed more of everything and that meant moving on from the premises that John at the bank had so generously provided less than a year after we opened there. I went back to my old habit of driving around the neighborhood, looking for a new home for DAMCO.

I found it in Watertown, a beautiful space five times the size of our original premises. It needed a lot of work to clean it up and make it habitable, but my small team and I tackled it over the course of a few weekends. As ever, I had leveraged all the cash I could get my hands on to buy the new machines I needed and pay for the extra staff. The moving costs we were facing were high, so when it came time to actually move the DAMCO plant across town into our new home, my first visit was to my bank.

I'd just moved my bank account to the local Watertown branch, so I had no idea how the meeting would go. If I'd still been with John, it would have been a formality—he probably would even have offered to come over and help move us himself—but my new guy, George Ginsberg, was a stranger to me. I decided to go prepared, taking my accounting statement along with me.

"Hmmm," said George as he leafed through the two pages that my accountant had just given me. There followed a long, awkward silence as George's eyes devoured the statements. There I was, waiting and sitting perfectly still and silent, like a school kid in the principal's office. I was missing John more than ever.

"Well," said George as he finally put the paper down on his desk, "you don't need my money."

"I'm sorry, sir, but I really do," I said, trying to keep my smile wide and my voice light. "We need $5,000 to move the plant. We're good to pay back the loan soon as well. It's all there for you to see."

"I'm sorry," said George. "I wasn't clear. You don't need to use the bank's money to pay your moving costs. You've got plenty of your own."

I shared a quick glance with George. I was starting to think this new guy was wired wrong.

"Let me explain," he said, showing me the statements with DAMCO's figures on it. "You see here? For the last six months, you've not been collecting your receivables, the money that people owe you for work carried out. It all adds up to something like $150,000. Why would you leave all that money out there? So, no, you don't need a loan from the bank—you need to go tell your customers to pay up."

It was an odd moment. I understood immediately what he meant, and I was delighted to discover there was so much money waiting to be collected. But it was a little embarrassing too. I knew how the situation was allowed to arise, and it was all on me. I assumed that people would pay their bills on time, and it hadn't occurred to me to check. I was so caught up with growing DAMCO that I neglected one of the most basic principles of business—collecting your accounts receivable.

I went back to the office and started calling my customers. They were all local, and most of them agreed to cut me a check right away and have it ready for me to collect as soon as I could pay them a visit. I did just that, and the next day I was back at the bank with an envelope full of checks, filling out my deposit slip.

"What do you want now, you damn Greek?"

I looked up and saw George walking over to me, a smile plastered all over his face.

"Just to deposit some checks I've been collecting."

"How much?"

It was my turn to smile. "About $85,000 worth."

"I should charge commission for the training I'm giving you," he joked. "But that's great. Really great. Remember: businesses need cash like the heart needs blood. Without it, nothing works."

Over the next several days, I worked my way through the list of late payments. Most of them came through quickly, but there was one company that was stubbornly resisting my attempts. I tried charm, humor, and even getting angry on the phone. Nothing worked. After two weeks of getting nowhere, I decided that I needed to escalate.

I left work on a Friday afternoon a little early with a cardboard box full of paperwork that I typically worked on at home. Only, instead of heading home, I drove to the Lexington Instrument Factory at the famous watch factory in Waltham, Massachusetts.

"Good afternoon," I said politely to the girl at reception, once I'd hefted my box in and placed it on the floor by a visitor's chair. "Can I see your CFO, please?"

"He's not in today."

"Okay. What about your treasurer? Can I meet with him instead, please?"

"He's just left for the weekend too."

"Fine," I said, sitting down and opening my box. "I'll wait." I pulled out some of my papers and started going through the hours of homework that I took back with me every weekend.

"Sir," the girl said, clearly starting to get a little anxious now. "You don't understand. Neither of them are here right now, and they won't be back in the office until Monday morning."

I nodded and smiled back. "That's fine. I understand. I'm happy to wait. I don't really have much choice anyway."

She looked confused.

"You see, your company owes my company $13,000 for a job we completed four months back. I've spent the last week on the phone with your accounts department trying to get them to pay, and nothing has worked. I need that $13,000 to pay my guys their wages this week. If I go back to the office without it, I'm pretty sure they'll lynch me. So, really, waiting here for the weekend is a much better option for me."

"But you can't wait here. The office is closing."

"Mine will permanently shut if I don't go back with that money."

I went back to my paperwork and waited to see what she would do next. I was calm, but my resolve had never been firmer. I was Plato all over again, and my fight for air was fierce.

"I'll call the police."

"Fine," I smiled. "I'll call the press. I'll tell them that right here in the heart of Waltham we have a business that refuses to pay for the work it orders and is willing to let others suffer as a result."

I returned my focus to my work and heard her huffing a little before she stepped out of reception through a door in the back.

Five or ten minutes passed, and she returned with a male colleague. He tried the same line about the police, but I stuck to my guns. I kept my tone polite and my request simple: "Just pay me what you owe me, and I'll be gone."

He left soon after, saying nothing.

Five minutes later somebody new came out and handed me a check. I looked at it, then I leaned over to hug him. It was the full amount.

———

Two years later, in May of 1970, my brother called to say our mother was in the hospital. The next day I took a plane to Greece.

I bought a bouquet of roses on the way to the hospital, and I presented them to her from her three granddaughters, including baby Marina, who had just been born in January. My mother was so excited and bragged to the other three ladies in the room about her American granddaughters.

The next morning my older brother was alone with our mother.

"I can't die now," she said.

"Why?"

"Because George came all the way here, and I don't want to get him upset and sad. I have to go after he leaves."

I stayed in Greece for more than three weeks. I left on a Thursday, and on the following Saturday morning, she passed away.

My mother was a very determined woman both in her early life and in her last days on this planet. She did exactly what she wanted to do, even during her last days and hours in this world.

She was, and she still is, my angel.

George E. Danis

# CHAPTER TEN
# DIFFICULT CHOICES

I WANTED TO EXPAND THE FACTORY YET AGAIN, but my staff and I decided the space we had wasn't nearly big enough. I went on the hunt for a bigger property and was just about to sign the lease to move out of Watertown when I received a letter from my landlord, Benjamin, asking me if I needed more space. He wrote that he was prepared to lease me some more or sell the whole building. I was both surprised and intrigued.

It was a dream come true. If I could stay, I wouldn't have to move all of the equipment and disrupt the whole operation. I called Benjamin and asked him the price.

"$275,000."

The building was built in the nineteenth century along the Charles River to serve the mill industry. It was 250,000 square feet, four stories high, old and dilapidated, and mostly empty. I wanted it.

But where was I going to find the $275,000? I immediately called my attorney to get his advice and started searching for a bank to loan me the money. Arlington Five Cents Savings came to my rescue, loaning me the money after they appraised the building. I started renovations within the first year and soon rented out the entire space. Eventually, I earned an award for renovation of the building on 5 Bridge Street. It was a win-win.

---

I sat in my office opposite one of our major customers and couldn't quite believe what I had just said nor could the man I was speaking with—a purchasing agent for one of the giants in the newly emerging tech industry. So I repeated it: "Paul, I don't know when your parts will be ready."

He looked confused the first time I'd said it, but now that he was hearing it for the second time, he appeared genuinely upset with me and jumped up.

"What do you mean you don't know?" he demanded. "You've got a bigger factory now, full of staff and machines down there, and it's noisy as hell. They must be doing something. How can you not know when they'll be finished on my jobs?"

I'd told him the truth so far, but now it was time to lie. I couldn't tell him that the plant was in a state of total chaos or that his was just one of many jobs that were cluttering up the manufacturing floor. I couldn't let him know that, after five years of incredible growth, DAMCO had gone from a sleek, well-run operation to a clunky, lumbering beast that wasn't performing at anything like its potential. "Leave it with me, Paul."

Paul left soon after, and I was stuck with the feeling that something had to change. DAMCO was about to enter its sixth year, and we had grown dramatically. We had clients throughout the northeast and down as far south as the Carolinas. We were generating significant profits and—just as significantly—were now collecting every cent we billed for. We increased our floor space by over fifty thousand square feet, purchased many newer, up-to-date machines, and hired new engineers and many new operators. Everyone was working diligently, but our planning and scheduling was dismal. Every time a customer told us they needed their job earlier or complained that theirs was late, we reordered our schedule. And whenever we got a new order from Motorola, Data General, or Western Electric, we changed it again. We lost priority, had no compass, and were discovering that all of our growth came at a cost. And the price was the chaos that we were living in now.

I knew what I had to do and where I needed to do it. I bought a plane ticket to Athens and told my staff that I was going back to the safe harbor where I grew up and made all my important decisions. "But I will be back in two weeks," I promised. "And I will have a full plan that will get us out of all this chaos."

They looked a little shocked.

"What are we supposed to do while you're away?" asked one of the managers.

I thought hard about my answer, hoping that I might come up with some words of wisdom that left them inspired and equipped to keep things going in my absence. But, as I opened my mouth, the only words that emerged were, "Just do whatever God guides you to do, and do whatever you can."

I arrived in Greece and headed straight for Karystos, where I holed myself up in a small apartment that I had purchased a few years back. When I spread out all of the papers that I brought with me, they covered the whole floor. The papers gave me a clear picture of pricing and work required for every job that we had taken on previously.

As I stared at the mess, I remembered each job, and the little apartment took on the same chaotic feeling as the factory floor. I finally understood what I had been seeing for months: our manufacturing floor wasn't organized appropriately to work at that kind of scale. We had no system other than each job being thrown into the already overloaded mix. Different jobs for different customers piled up alongside each other. It was inefficient, unreliable, and vulnerable to all kinds of delays and disruptions.

All this I knew deep down already. But looking at the papers, ignoring my brothers' invitations to go out to eat with them and spend precious time with my Greek family, I finally had the opportunity and the resolve to do something about it. I was determined not to leave the apartment until I had fixed it.

In the end it took me only a week. After seven days of staring intensely at figures, of endless calculations of time and price, of trying to clear my eyes and my thoughts of every preconceived notion of how things *should* and *must* be done,

George E. Danis

I finally had a working solution. I saw jobs differently: as a series of individual unique steps that needed to be completed before another job could begin. I broke the factory down into ten different departments, each with its own sub-steps and stages, and designed a system that would allow the most efficient use of machines possible. This system would not allow jobs to pile up like rush-hour traffic on a busy turnpike but instead would ensure that everything within the factory was constantly flowing.

After spending the next week with my family, I flew back to Boston and gathered my team. I told them about my plan and how I was convinced that it was going to make our work so much better. I developed detailed spreadsheets that mapped the steps required for each customer order, with particular attention paid to the time we needed to allot. I knew exactly how many hours it would take for each job to go from start to finish and was convinced that this was the key to fixing our problem.

Immediately, we stopped working on some of the jobs that were down on the floor and put into action the plan for this more streamlined, efficient system where we started one job at a time and took each one right through all the departments at the same time. It worked, and within a month our plant was transformed. Paul got his parts, and every other client got theirs, too. When Paul visited me again, he asked me what changed, and I told him I had developed a "choo-choo train system." I wasn't the only one trying to find new ways of improving efficiency. Within a year the business world was talking about a new innovation to emerge from Japan called "just-in-time" production.

Fixing our approach to production allowed DAMCO to really take off. In 1974 we made something in the region of over $6.5 million. It was a lot of money, but I didn't feel as though I'd finally become a success in business. The truth is that in business I've never felt like I've made it—whatever that means. I've always wanted to be the best supplier that I can be, and there is always something new to learn or some vital way to improve. It's like life itself: we should never allow our hunger for knowledge to fade and die. We should always be open to the next thing that we can learn.

When I was just about to start DAMCO, I met with a friend from Honeywell. Bernie was a legend in the plant and was the kind of man who always had a wise word that was perfect for the occasion. I was hoping for a little of that wisdom when I told him I was planning on starting my own business.

"Why do you want to start your own business, George?"

"That's easy," I said. "I love building things, and I love to have people working with me. Owning my own business is something that I always dreamed of doing."

"Good," he said.

"Why did you ask me that?"

"Because if you had told me that your aim was to make money, I would have told you to forget all about it. Nobody ever makes it in business when they set out to get rich. But starting a business because you're curious and want to have others join you, that's a great place to start."

Bernie wasn't Greek, but his outlook on life was just the same as the view shared by the villagers I grew up among. I was brought up with the Greek belief that the way to get the most out of life is to enjoy its successes in moderation, and nothing for me has really changed since then. I want to live well within my means, so I keep my tastes simple and my happiness levels high.

Even today, the only financial goal I'm ever interested in hitting each year is covering costs. Anything material on top of that is a bonus. The other goals are the ones that I am really interested in: Are the businesses the best they can be? Are my factories the ones that people most want to work in? Does my staff feel appreciated and rewarded? Do I treat them like they are family? Do I know all their names? Do I know their families? Do we eat together regularly and enjoy family barbecues and fun days together?

I'm proud that my staff is getting the best pay in the industry. They have great 401Ks, the best health and dental coverage, the most paid holidays, and every quarter they get an extra week's pay as bonus. It's little wonder that they bring their best efforts to their job. Always my people come first.

That's what success is to me. It couldn't have less to do with the cars in the garage or the zeros on the bank balance. It's about creating opportunities for as many people as possible to come to work knowing they will be valued and rewarded.

Despite the improvements we made to our systems, not everything was going well. At this time our controller,

Mike, was not paying attention to details. He was failing to deposit the payroll withholding taxes to the IRS, and I was totally unaware of it. I was reviewing the business accounts and saw they were high, so I started giving extra bonuses to our people. The IRS continued to inquire about our tax deposits, and Mike continued to ignore them. Soon the IRS showed up at the reception desk. Mike had taken the day off, knowing that they were coming to see us, so it was left to me to see them.

I invited them into my office, and they served the notice that we had failed to deposit close to $1 million in payroll tax withholdings. It was a shock, and I was aware of some distant urge within me to panic, but fear was not an option. I needed to act. I apologized and immediately had our payroll department manager review our cash availability to pay the IRS. Unfortunately, we didn't have the million dollars available. However, I negotiated with the IRS, and we paid in installments for the next three months with a penalty and interest. This was an important lesson in owning your own business: always be aware, always analyze, and always review everyone's tasks in detail. As the saying goes, the devil is in the details. Lesson learned.

That year, 1974, was full of essential lessons. As well as reconfiguring the way the plant was run, I discovered what it was like to be a business owner when the financial markets are in free fall. It all started with the 1973 oil crisis, which in turn led to a bear market through 1974. The Dow lost almost half its value, and businesses were panicked. As the pressure mounted and the numbers tightened, I did everything I could to make sure we were as efficient as possible by cutting any expenditure that wasn't necessary.

I also learned to take a clear look at DAMCO, assessing at what point I would need to cut staff and who should go. It wasn't easy to think like this. We felt more like a family than a business, and the idea of letting anyone go pained me. But as the economy slowed and inflation rose, I knew that there might be a point when the financial numbers would force me to act, and I would have to lose a few employees to keep the rest.

Those kinds of decisions are never easy, but they are precisely the times when you need to step up as a leader, and being prepared is vital. You don't want to make decisions about who stays and who goes when you're deep in the middle of a crisis and the stresses are enormous. You want to decide in advance, to know how you will deal with a crisis way before it hits.

Luckily, we rode it out. DAMCO emerged from the 1974 crash with our reserves depleted and our orders down but all our staff and team completely intact. And as the crisis eased and the numbers turned up again, I was restless for growth. It was time to start another business.

Though we were supplying metal casings for computers, I noticed that many of our customers were asking us for smaller items as well, such as nuts, bolts, and screws. Western Electric, AT&T, General Electric, and others couldn't get their hands on the fastenings required to fit their various components in place, and they were often complaining about how hard it was for them to find reliable distributors. It was a clear gap in the market and one I intended to fill.

The first challenge was the name. I'd liked DAMCO a lot when I first chose it, but I was now seeing the drawbacks in a word that had no clear meaning to potential customers and that led to many jokingly called it "Dam Co." I decided not to make the same mistake twice and opted for a name that summed up exactly what we did: Fastener Supply.

The plan was simple: we would be nothing more than a distributor. Once I had chosen a member of the DAMCO team to run it and leased a warehouse to house the stock, I began the process of removing myself from the daily running of the company. It was a deliberate choice and one that I still practice today. I have never wanted to be the kind of business owner who doesn't allow people to flourish. Instead, I have taken my inspiration from people like Fred, Mr. Contos, and Captain Manoli. Even though one was in manufacturing, the other in hospitality, and the other in shipping, all of them shared the same essential trait as managers. They gave their staff all the tools and support they needed to succeed, then stood back and let them have at it. I hadn't been able to do it from the start at DAMCO, so with this new company I wanted to get it right from the very beginning.

A couple of years into this new venture, I was told that there was a crisis I needed to deal with. "We need a bigger warehouse," my manager told me. "We haven't got room for all this inventory. That's why we keep losing money month after month."

His words gave me the chills. Ever since making the successful changes to our processes at DAMCO, I developed a strong dislike of seeing products gathering dust anywhere in my business. I liked motion and efficiency and the sense that things were moving through our systems as quickly as possible. As far as I was concerned, if Fastener Supply wanted a bigger warehouse because they had too much inventory, it couldn't be good.

The manager's request for more space came just before he went on a month's vacation, so I took the opportunity to visit the warehouse in his absence. It was worse than I feared.

The guy I had chosen to manage the company was one of my salesmen at DAMCO, and I assumed that since he knew how to sell, he must also know how to correctly price his products. He didn't. He set his prices shockingly low—just 15 percent above what he was paying his suppliers. To make matters worse, the price he was paying those suppliers was for bulk orders, but his customers were buying the fasteners, nuts, and bolts in such small quantities that he was swimming in stock. The warehouse was full of inventory that was gathering dust—money we spent out that was not being turned into income.

I remembered the advice of George, the bank manager, who had told me about cash being the lifeblood of any business. As I looked around Fastener Supply, it was obvious that there was too little blood and too weak a heart to get things going.

After I toured the warehouse and took a good look at the books, I sat in my manager's office with his assistants and told them what I thought. "We don't need a bigger warehouse with more inventory. We need a smaller one with less."

They were surprised and a little shocked, but I pressed on. I took a look at all the purchase orders and called the financial controller to give me an analysis of the associated costs required to run the business. He came back soon enough with a figure, and together we worked out that for us to administer a job from A to Z, we would need to add 35 percent to whatever we were paying our supplier, and that wasn't even allowing for any profit—which I set at 20 percent.

"Listen," I said to the whole staff when I arrived at the warehouse the next day and called them into a meeting, "from now on, things are going to change. First, we're only ever going to buy the minimum quantity that the supplier is willing to sell us. That same quantity is the minimum order size that we're going to sell to our customers. And if the customer wants only a fraction of the supplier's minimum quantity, they're still going to have to pay for the whole lot. There will be no more filling these shelves with leftovers from what we've bought from our suppliers. We're going to order only when a customer has placed their order too. And then there's the pricing."

I paused. They all looked stunned.

"Our stock is going to become a lot more expensive. Instead of adding 15 percent to the order, it'll be 55 percent."

The sales team took it the worst. "We're not going to be able to sell it to anybody at all!"

"Think about it this way," I said. "Every sale you do make will generate profit. And if you don't sell anything, at least it won't be costing us money like it is now. For once in this company's history, we'll be ahead of the game."

There was a lot of grumbling, which I understood. There was even talk about giving up, which got me riled.

"You don't give up in business! You dig in and figure out what it will take to become more resourceful and more persuasive as a salesperson. You got big sales with those low prices before—that was easy. Now it's time to get better at your job, to find out how good at sales you really are."

By the time the manager returned from vacation, the grumbling had stopped and the new pricing system was in place. Sales had halved, just as we all knew they would, but we were finally on the way to being profitable for the first time in our four-year history. Soon it was well on its way to becoming the most profitable company I have ever owned.

---

Everything has a cost. Being disorganized in your workflow has a cost. Setting your prices too low has a cost. Leaving inventory on a warehouse shelf has a cost. And being so devoted to the business that you lose sight of your family, that has the greatest cost of all.

After Stella and Barbara, Kathy and I had had two more daughters: Marina and Jennifer. Our family of six was complete around the time Fastener Supply was finally getting on its feet, but this was also the point at which my marriage to

Kathy was starting to choke.

I loved being a father. My daughters were, and always have been, my greatest joy, and I loved the time I spent with them. Whether I was driving them to school in the mornings or sitting around at home on the weekends, seeing each of them grow into their unique characters day by day, week by week, was a privilege. But I did not spend enough time with them. I was rarely home in the evenings to eat with the family, and I was often visiting customers out of state and had to stay away overnight.

I knew that I was not putting in as much time at home as I wanted, but I was also determined to build the businesses and be able to provide the girls with the very best start in life that I could. I built many houses—partly because I enjoyed designing them but mainly to accommodate our ever-changing needs as they grew bigger—and I strove to give our children the best education possible. Even though it was a world away from the village of Mili, where six of us crammed into our two-room house and walked barefoot to school, my values were the same as those of my parents. Like them, I wanted to provide a good home and to instill in my children a love of learning and a hunger for education.

Kathy and I disagreed often. She wasn't interested in moving to bigger homes and didn't relish the challenge of starting again and again in new neighborhoods. This clashed with my lack of sentimental attachment to our homes and my restlessness to take on new building projects. We disagreed about education too. Kathy grew up in a family that saw things differently from mine, and my insistence that the girls all go to college was another point we argued about.

Eventually, we reached a crisis point and agreed that I should move out. I took an apartment just next door to the DAMCO office, just a mile and a half from the family home. I still took the girls to school in the morning and spent time with all of them on weekends. I would accompany Kathy and the girls to church and attend social events. Kathy and I even used to vacation together every year in the Caribbean in the winter, with three other couples, and in Greece in the summer. Apart from the girls, nobody knew we had separated. In many ways very little changed in our lives, and we found a balance in our relationship that had been missing for years.

I am grateful that we found our compromise, but even to this day I feel the sting of regret about the breakdown of our marriage. I took my vows seriously, and it was painful to see us both caught up in a struggle like that.

In spite of the stress of balancing work and home, our family spent many good times together—especially in Greece. Every summer, as soon as school was out, we would all board a plane for Athens, take the short ferry ride from Rafina over to the island of Evia, and drive the few miles down the coast to Karystos. In less than twelve hours, we transitioned from the world of Boston—with its routines and rules and seemingly endless demands on our time, a world in which my restlessness and curiosity found a constant supply of opportunities to pursue—to the world of Karystos. There, with the village of Mili behind us, nestled at the base of

Mount Ohi, and the clear waters of the Aegean sparkling before us, everything was different.

Everything slowed.

There were no plans made weeks in advance. There was no complicated schedule of rides to be given, events to attend, or errands to be run. There was just a series of days made up of swimming in the ocean, lazing in the sun, and enjoying the never-ending stream of family and friends who were on hand for meals and conversations. We ate lunches where the table groaned under the weight of platters of fresh fish, bowls of tomatoes so fragrant you'd think they were flowers, and baked cheese and spinach pita so good you couldn't stop eating even though you were full long ago. We'd sleep in the afternoon, then, when the night was cool and the clock approached ten, we'd head back down to the little harbor and the string of restaurants overlooking the water. There would be more friends, more family, more food, and more laughter as we whiled away the final hours of the day.

Only at night, when everyone was asleep, would I allow my thoughts to return to work. I would make phone calls and deal with any problems that had come up, but mostly I kept my summers in Karystos free from the pressures of business. It took a little discipline on my part to leave it all behind, but from the first days of DAMCO, I always wanted my businesses to be able to function without me. This wasn't about a lack of interest on my part but a desire to ensure that everything I took on was in the best possible position to grow. If a business could only function on a daily basis with me at a desk calling the shots, it was never going to fulfill its true potential. The goal was always for my businesses to be designed to flourish without me. Taking a long vacation eight time zones away every year was a great way of checking how empowered and equipped my team was to run things in my absence.

The girls spoke little Greek, but with their Greek cousins Mary, George, Stella, and Xristos, they never struggled to communicate. They'd all speak their own mix of Greek and English, laughing often and enjoying the freedom of a life in a small Greek town. Day by day the girls' skin would turn darker and darker shades of olive brown, and I could feel myself recharging too. The warmth, the peace, the people, the sense of being known and loved and still belonging even after I'd made my home an ocean away—it all helped heal us and make us feel whole again.

We were like trees returned to the forest. The soil, the air, the sun all nourished us. We'd stay in Greece as long as we possibly could, often returning home the day before school resumed. They were not just good times. They were the best times.

## CHAPTER ELEVEN
# USING YOUR VOICE

MY INTEREST IN POLITICS didn't begin the day Senator John F. Kennedy visited me in the Charles Street Jail. Even before I boarded the *Atlantic Sea* and began my long journey to America, I was fascinated by politics and fully committed to the idea that if we want to see anything change in the way we are governed, we must be involved ourselves. Like almost every other Greek person I know, I learned this as a child. Whenever we were eating together as a family, the conversation would inevitably be centered on politics, whether it was at the local, village, national, or international level. But my parents didn't just talk, they acted. My mother devoted herself to the work of the church in our local community, and my father was elected to local office in the village. Both were motivated by a simple but vital desire to help others in need and create a better community for all. It was politics reduced to its purest form.

By the time I received my green card in 1961, I was keen to do the same in the United States. Building successful businesses was a way of impacting the lives of individuals, but I was also interested in the bigger picture. I wanted to meet political leaders and support those who I thought were building a better, fairer society.

It wasn't hard to do it. The Greek community, wherever they are in the world, likes to be involved in politics, so it was unsurprising that the Greek community ended up serving as my doorway to meeting political leaders. From the earliest days of DAMCO, I joined with the philanthropic efforts of local Greek businesses, and it was through this work that I met Michael Dukakis. He was a state representative at the time, but in 1972 he ran—unsuccessfully—for lieutenant governor with Kevin White. Despite the loss, Michael made a good impression on the Democratic Party and on me as well. By the time he received the nomination for governor in 1974, he and I had become close, and I was taking on the role of unofficial campaign advisor on budgets and other programs. Michael is a pure liberal through and through, while I'm just a social liberal and an economic conservative, who believes in fiscal moderation. We didn't agree on everything, but that worked just fine for both of us.

While Michael was running—successfully this time—for governor, something happened that made it even more important that I become involved in politics. It was July 1974, and Kathy, the girls, and I were spending it, as usual, in Karystos. I made a rare but brief trip back to Boston to cochair the national convention of AHEPA. I'd been involved as a member with them since 1966, and 1974 was the first year that I was elected to cochair the convention. I wouldn't have left Karystos for anything else. The rest of the family stayed in Greece without me.

The week of the convention, the United States was in a constitutional crisis with the resignation of President Richard Nixon, and Turkey took the opportunity and invaded the island of Cyprus. It was a shocking escalation of events, and like the rest of my fellow countrymen, I was concerned for the safety and well-being of the thriving Greek community that had lived on Cyprus for generations. There were rumors of atrocities, and by the time the AHEPA convention started, the mood among the seven thousand delegates was wild and concerning: we wanted the world to know what was going on in Cyprus, and we wanted America to intervene to prevent more bloodshed and protect the rights of our people living there. It was a full-blown international crisis. Politics had never felt so important.

The challenge was clear: the press was giving only minimal coverage to the story, so it was up to us to raise public awareness about what was going on. We called on the government to use sanctions to force Turkey out and organized big demonstrations in Washington. I even had half a million bumper stickers printed with the words "Turkey: Get Out Of Cyprus." I handed them out to AHEPA delegates from all over the country.

That was the first political campaign within the Greek community to use bumper stickers, and they were a huge hit. Even in the late 1980s, I still saw them on the roads as I was traveling with Governor Dukakis across the country. In many ways, it was ridiculous that we had to resort to something as basic as bumper stickers to raise public awareness of what Turkey was doing in Cyprus. The press exists to inform us, yet in the summer of 1974, they were collectively obsessed with our own constitutional crisis as Nixon fought to avoid impeachment. Don't get me wrong, that was a genuine domestic crisis about which the people needed to be fully informed, but the events in Cyprus were not just another niche news story that belonged on the other side of the ocean. It was an act of aggression that violated the rights and freedoms of lawful civilians. It was a land grab, the likes of which we would see again decades later in Kuwait by Saddam Hussein and in Crimea by Russia. When totalitarian leaders see their peers acting without consequence while the West gazes inward, those regimes only become more emboldened.

The bumper stickers helped raise awareness, but it was still difficult to persuade the politicians to act. In the end, we did not get what we wanted in Cyprus. Secretary of State Kissinger declared that we would not do anything against Turkey, and in many ways that policy continues today, almost fifty years later. Turkey learned back in '74 that the United States was not interested in conflict, nor were we interested in democratic fairness. Today, we have spent billions of dollars trying to get the Russians out of Ukraine, rightfully so, but we need to be fair to more countries like Cyprus as well. I fear that one day we might come to regret that.

---

George E. Danis

In spite of the lack of any significant political outcome, the campaign felt like a success to me personally. It confirmed my conviction that being a full citizen of a country requires some degree of political engagement and strengthened my belief that in the United States it is possible for anyone—even a formerly illegal immigrant like me—to become involved.

That summer I also learned that trying to persuade the government to change course on any issue is tough, especially when our system is designed in such a way that politicians are always focusing on reelection. This breeds a shortsighted mindset, with so much of our elected officials' time and energy taken up with fundraising and trying to secure their own political futures rather than do their job.

So many of our problems today need more than just two, four, or six years in order to fix them. When it comes to problems like the climate and trade, we need solutions that are going to take decades to implement. We need policies that are bigger than party politics and politicians who are willing to care about more than securing their own standing in their party. As citizens we must move from seeing politics as a spectator sport to viewing it as a forum in which we can all participate. We need to become a lot more politically involved than we have been over recent years, reminding our leaders of the issues we care about and the consequences to their time in office if they ignore us.

———

After all the turmoil of 1974—the financial pressures on the businesses, the difficulties that Kathy and I were experiencing, and everything else—I began to develop an even greater appetite for politics. Working alongside Mike Dukakis during his gubernatorial campaign in 1974 was a pleasure, and I was eager to join in another campaign just as soon as the right candidate and the right race came along. Unfortunately, in 1978 Dukakis lost the nomination of the Democratic Party to Governor Edward King, who went on to be elected governor later that year.

When I met Paul Tsongas, I knew he was the man I wanted to support next. His father was a Greek immigrant who had become a successful businessman, and Paul and I saw many issues the same way. He was significantly more moderate on economic matters than most Massachusetts Democrats. I liked that and was happy to do what I could to help him run for the Senate in 1978.

Paul and I spent a lot of time together during that campaign, and we toured the state, meeting potential voters. We made a habit of visiting manufacturing factories at the end of a shift, greeting the workers as they came out. Even though he had been a city councilor, a county commissioner, and a two-term congressman, Paul wasn't widely recognized. He was also a lot shorter than me, and often as we stood and talked with the flow of workers about the issues concerning them, people mistook me for the candidate, shaking my hand first. Paul took it in good humor and would often tell me that we should swap roles. "George, maybe I should go home and you should campaign for me. You'd win the election!"

In the end Paul didn't need to deceive anyone to win. He was elected to the United States Senate and beat the sitting Republican by ten points. He was a great senator, but toward the end of his first term, he was diagnosed with non-Hodgkin lymphoma. He retired in 1983.

Dukakis went on to challenge Edward King. He won the nomination and got elected governor again in 1982, this time with John Kerry as the lieutenant governor. Dukakis appointed Kerry to the Senate seat when Paul resigned.

Later, after Paul had made a full recovery, Paul was the first Democrat to launch his bid for the 1992 presidential election and the only candidate to discuss the federal deficit as a serious issue. I went back and supported him by raising money across the country for his campaign. At his first speech at the National Press Club in Washington, D.C., Paul told a joke about a man who falls over a cliff in the Grand Canyon.

"He's clinging to a tree, scared to death, and calls up for help. He's shocked and relieved when a voice responds. It tells him, 'Don't be afraid. Just let go, and I'll help you.' The man thinks for a moment, then yells out, 'Uh, is there anyone else out there?'"

Paul understood the extent to which many in the United States were dissatisfied with the political choices offered. They wanted someone else, and Paul was willing to be that person. Two weeks later I took him to Columbus, Ohio, then on to Philadelphia and New Jersey, raising money from the Greek communities in those states. By the end of

Super Tuesday, he'd all but lost to Bill Clinton, but I thought then, and I still think now, that Paul Tsongas always had the potential to be the kind of politician that this country needs. He was clear to the point of being blunt, and he always refused to sweeten his economic policies with short-term sugar hits in an attempt to win a few extra votes. He remained extremely popular in Massachusetts until his early death in 1997, aged just fifty-five. If cancer hadn't plagued him, I sometimes wonder how different the country might be today.

Despite the fact that I supported both Dukakis and Tsongas in their respective campaigns, I never registered as a Democrat. I have always registered as an Independent. It is my belief that being an Independent allows you to take a step back from the inward focus of party politics and the pursuit of a certain prescribed ideology. In business you have to be flexible in order to survive, responding to the constantly shifting needs and desires of your customers. How much more so is that true of politics? Being Independent allows you to focus more on what is best for the country itself.

Perhaps it's not surprising that I would want to take such a high view of politics. Greece became the birthplace of democracy in the year 507 B.C., with the introduction of an innovative set of political reforms. It was called *demokratia* and meant "rule by the people" (taken from the words for "the people," *demos*, and "power," *kratos*). The world had known nothing like it, and its influence has lasted for millennia—it has even been suggested that the political divide between left and right that characterizes so many democracies today

George E. Danis

can trace its roots to the liberal views of Athenians and the conservative opinions of the Spartans.

At home in the village and down in Karystos, politics was—and still is today—a constant topic of conversation, but not the kind of political discussion that is thinly veiled entertainment. Greeks love nothing better than to talk about politics, but it rarely involves gossiping about who is going to gain power, who is losing power, or who might find themselves embarrassed by some political scandal. I was brought up in a family that did not pledge allegiance to a particular party and blindly follow it like it was our favorite sports team.

When we talked about politics, we talked about the impact it had on the people we knew and lived among, and it is still largely true today. Policies are evaluated on the basis of how they will change real lives of real people, not on how many votes they will win or points they will score. We talk about people because at the end of the day, we know that politics is nothing without them. Politics is the tool by which we nurture, develop, and protect our society. We, the people, are the body that politics serves, not the other way around.

We need help today. As I look around me, I am convinced that we have lost our way. Politics seems to be removed from its primary purpose, and people seem to have lost their appetite for engaging as citizens. There's so much yelling that the bulk of us just want to switch off, and there's too little humility from our leaders to truly listen to what people really want to discuss. Compromise has become a dirty word, along with others like bipartisanship, unity, and reform. As an Independent I see fault on both sides, which is nothing new. But what troubles me is that I see too few people on either side of the political debate who are breaking the mold and making a difference.

George E. Danis

# CHAPTER TWELVE
# CARTER, CYPRUS, AND AMERICAN EXCEPTIONALISM

FROM THE MOMENT I ARRIVED at the White House and was ushered toward the Oval Office, I was battling my thoughts. Part of me was obsessed with my surroundings. The strength of the security presence, the wealth and clear opulence of the building, the quiet corridors lined with portraits of former presidents all fascinated me, and I was tempted to feel overwhelmed about being invited inside. But I needed to be totally clear in my focus. This was an opportunity unlike any I'd ever had before. If I didn't grasp it with both hands, it wouldn't just be me who'd regret it: a whole community of tens and tens of thousands of people might mourn this missed opportunity.

I first met Jimmy Carter when he was campaigning for the Democratic nomination in 1976. The world continued to spiral since 1974, with the Middle East and Soviet Union both brewing trouble. I wasn't alone in thinking that President Ford was not up to the job, and when my friends and I met

Jimmy Carter in New Hampshire with Chris, a friend who was a state representative, I was struck by Carter's approach. He was calm and measured, and he appeared to be signed up to the idea of leveling the playing field in terms of democracy.

Instead of allowing autocratic regimes to take the upper hand, it seemed to me that a Carter presidency would defend the vulnerable in the face of tyranny. He even went so far as to say, while campaigning for president, that he would get Turkey to withdraw from Cyprus. As soon as I'd heard that, I was sold.

It wasn't too long after the inauguration that I joined with a handful of other supporters from the Greek community and traveled to meet with President Carter at the White House. We were excited to be there but all knew how high the stakes were that day. If we could press Carter to make good on his promise to push Turkey out of Cyprus, then our visit would be worthwhile.

From the moment we were shown into the Oval Office and were invited to sit down by the president, it was clear that the promise to deal with Turkey was off the table.

"There's nothing I can do," Carter said. "The Turks are not budging."

We were upset, but it changed nothing. The pledge that helped secure our support when Carter was campaigning came to nothing. None of us were surprised at the time, and certainly we weren't as the Carter presidency evolved.

He made some particularly bad decisions around the 1978 Olympics in Moscow. The Soviets had invaded

Afghanistan, and Carter made the decision to boycott the games in protest. Another leader might have decided to see the Olympics for what they are: an opportunity to deepen the ties of global unity and celebrate our shared humanity. But Carter wanted to use the event for political gain. He got nothing. America stayed away from the party, and the Soviets stayed in Afghanistan.

Between the continuing economic recession, the energy crisis, and the Iran hostage crisis, Carter became known as a man who couldn't get things done. I liked him personally, but those four years were one crisis after another.

As the end of his first term came into view, there wasn't universal confidence among his former supporters that President Carter would be able to win again. His approval ratings were low, and people started talking about who else within the Democratic Party would make a better candidate. Massachusetts Senator Ted Kennedy's name came up more and more in conversation.

I'd met Senator Kennedy many times, and he had become a good friend. When he decided to run against President Carter, I was all for it, and I set out with others to raise money from the Greek community. From New York to California, Chicago and Detroit to Atlanta, we found people eager to support the senator in his bid for the Democratic nomination. His policies were popular and his position on Cyprus was clear. We liked him and wanted him to go all the way. We raised a lot of money for him.

However, there was no way that President Carter was

going to roll over and simply hand Kennedy the nomination. He fought back, and for a while I felt like I was going to get caught in the crossfire.

Things peaked around the time of Senator Kennedy's birthday. I was helping to organize an evening fundraiser to celebrate and met with the senator a week before to go through the final details. To my surprise, Senator Kennedy told me that the vice president, Walter Mondale, had invited himself along to the event.

"I'd like him to sit with you at your table," the senator said to me. There wasn't much else I could say other than yes.

On that night, I spent almost two hours talking with the vice president. We covered the Middle East, and I was sure to spend a lot of time talking about Cyprus. We also discussed the economic situation at the time (interest rates and inflation were both high), the aftermath of the Vietnam War, and where the country might go next. It was a moment that I wanted to savor. I'd come a long way from the village, and now I was sitting beside the vice president, talking like this.

We were able to get over 750 guests to attend—most of them Greek—and the vice president was planning on getting up and saying a few words to them.

"Well," he said a few minutes before he was due to speak, "what do I tell them?"

I guess I could have shrugged and batted the question away. I could have suggested he echo President Carter's words in the Oval Office and tell the crowd there was nothing he could do about Turkey. But I didn't want to score any cheap points. I still genuinely wanted the administration to get tough on Turkey and wanted the vice president to see that there was a lot of support for the idea. So I told him to lie.

"Just tell them that you're working toward a solution on Cyprus."

He said just that. It got him a long round of applause, the biggest of his speech. I knew that the words were hollow, that he was giving people the impression that he was outlining policy when in reality he was just looking for a good line to build up to in a speech. But I'd spent enough time in politics by then to see behind the mask.

"How did I do?" he asked when he sat back down beside me.

"Very well, Mr. Vice President."

I looked up and saw Senator Kennedy walking over. This time I was in no doubt about what I should do. I quickly excused myself and left them to it. The convention in New York was the end of the Kennedy candidacy.

---

The year 1980 ended with the presidency shifting from Carter to Reagan. The Iranians released the hostages, but things in South and Central America descended into the chaos of revolution. It wasn't a great first term, but President Reagan managed to secure a second. Unsurprisingly, for a man whose previous career had been in Hollywood, Reagan was a strong communicator. People warmed to him, and in the process, the public appetite for a new type of politician grew even stronger. Ideology was not the only battleground on which a president would have to succeed. Communication mattered just as much.

The whole episode of my attempts to persuade the government to act tough on Turkey brought my thoughts into focus. Over the years they have continued to evolve.

I believe that U.S. foreign policy has been misguided for far too long, starting in 1950 when President Truman sent troops to Korea and continuing through when Presidents Eisenhower, Kennedy, and then Johnson all escalated U.S. involvement in Vietnam. Their policies meddled in conflicts that we had no business involving ourselves in. And when our leaders realized this fact and decided to withdraw, the speed and the manner of those withdrawals were so poorly planned and executed that they made bad situations even worse.

Since I first became involved in politics, I have seen several U.S. leaders make terrible decisions over who to support. From Panamanian dictator Manuel Noriega to Osama bin Laden, the CIA has been involved in conflicts that that have destabilized regions, cost countless lives, and amassed debts in the trillions of dollars. Of course, the Taliban, Saddam Hussein, and Qaddafi were no saints, and the people they brutalized deserved better, but there has been a deep hypocrisy in foreign policy over the years: we will shed blood to depose some of these despots, while other regimes guilty of horrendous human rights violations—in China, Turkey, and Saudi Arabia—get our warm handshakes and our business.

Sadly, the issue of Turkey's involvement in Cyprus has

been ignored for over forty-five years. The Turkish government has taken note and is continuously harassing the Greek islands with military overflights. Cyprus itself remains divided, with the Turkish-occupied half economically depressed, while the Republic of Cyprus—the independent half—has thrived and become a full member of the European Union.

I have attended many forums where the subject of American exceptionalism has been the central focus. Whenever I hear people arguing that America has a duty to act as the world's policeman, my mind turns to the domestic ills that our leaders would rather sweep under the carpet: the poverty experienced by people living in cities like Detroit, the fact that since 1960 the median wealth of white households has tripled while the wealth of Black households has barely increased, or the fact that for decades the unemployment rate among Black Americans has been roughly twice that of white Americans. How can we save the world's problems when we have failed for generations to deal with our own?

We can do so much better when it comes to health care. The costs are becoming difficult to sustain, but I believe there are solutions that our leaders could turn to that would make significant improvements. For example, we currently have a shortage of doctors, yet we have hundreds of medical schools. The acceptance rate for those medical schools is in the region of 5 percent. That's too low, and it is creating a serious resource problem that affects us all—just recently, after suffering from a bout of pneumonia while I was in Greece, I tried to book an appointment with my doctor back home in the United States. The earliest appointment I could get was twelve months out.

My advice would be for the government to mandate medical schools to increase their acceptance rate to 15 or 20 percent. Those that don't comply would lose their tax-free status and see a restriction of government subsidies on their research. Is this a policy of the right or the left? I don't know, and frankly, I don't much care!

It could take years before the increased number of health-care workers make a significant impact on our everyday experiences of health care, but if we don't do something drastic now, the best we can hope for is for the situation to stay the same. In reality, it's going to get a whole lot worse: the number of over sixty-fives is set to double by 2050, and our aging population will place even more strain on our limited health-care resources.

I'd also suggest that we look again at the pharmaceutical industry. As a collective it is guilty of mismanaging enormous amounts of money, and those costs are skyrocketing. What do we do about it? Nothing. We just accept it. We accept that the era of hospitals being nonprofit and well-regulated is in the past, and that from now on the only way forward is to establish private hospitals that are publicly traded. It's not working. The free market is great at driving innovation in industry or rewarding excellence in other areas, but when it comes to the drugs we all rely on to stay alive, the pursuit of profit makes everything too murky.

Politicians are little better than Big Pharma. They see the

political capital on offer in the health-care system, and they use it to their own ends. The so-called Affordable Care Act was a case in point. With a little adaptation to extend coverage to the unemployed, Medicaid was a perfectly viable option. From there, the government needed to mandate that all employers must provide health care for their people. Making the system more affordable and simpler to navigate would have changed health care for the better, bringing it into line with the quality of care available in other developed nations.

None of this is complicated, but it is all too controversial for our current political leaders. They have become communicators first and problem-solvers second. We are being run by a bunch of salespeople, when what we really need in serious times like these are leaders with the skills of an engineer. We need people who are committed to solving problems, not dealing in distractions.

————————

The land of my birth has seen firsthand the consequence of American exceptionalism. The disastrous withdrawal from Afghanistan in 2021, the failure to react when Assad in Syria crossed our so-called red lines, the inability to defeat ISIS as they rampaged throughout 2015 and 2016, these all contributed to the mass exodus of so many people as they fled to Europe in hopes of safety. Many put themselves in the hands of criminals and climbed into overcrowded, unsafe rubber boats and tried to cross from Turkey into Greece. Many died. It has fallen to Greece to act as a landing stage for its neighbors, with too little support from Europe.

We need to figure out what America's place in the world will look like for the rest of the twenty-first century. We are no longer the world's policeman, but there is more to being a leader than acting as an enforcer. We can use our power and experience to foster democracy in other countries. We can encourage nations that level their own playing fields and nurture citizenship. We can choose not to line our pockets by turning a blind eye to dictators and autocrats. We can have integrity and justice at the heart of our foreign policy, and the world will be better for it.

How do we do that? The answer lies with us, the citizens. We need to demand that our congressmen and congresswomen represent our views. We need to make ourselves known to our senators. We need to organize our communities around the issues that we care about. We need to lobby where necessary and not be dissuaded by those who consider ours to be a minority view, and we need to be prepared to dig in for the long haul. Most of all, we need to remember this one thing about our politicians: they work for us.

Senator Kennedy never forgot me and included me in many of his local meetings, including dinners at his home in Hyannis Port, Massachusetts. He also asked me to represent him on an official visit to Greece from the president of the United States in 1999, Bill Clinton. I received security clearance, and I became a member of the planning committee for the visit, participating in numerous conference calls with U.S. ambassadors to NATO, including the U.S. ambassador to Greece, as well as many of the Greek foreign ministry experts. It was a unique experience and a wonderful insight into the inner circles of government, especially relating to communications and planning. It was a dream come true.

Despite the planning, even before the trip began there was trouble. There were demonstrations all over Athens by the Greek public, especially the left wing of the political parties, and at one of the demonstrations, they burned an effigy of President Clinton. We had to postpone the trip for two weeks due to the upheaval and unrest, but Clinton was determined to visit Greece no matter what.

By the time we arrived in Greece, the atmosphere had calmed. I was one of the guests attending the state dinner held by the president of Greece and the Greek government. President Stephanopoulos spoke first, lecturing President Clinton about the history of America and how it had mishandled the dictatorship government of Greece during the junta in the sixties, reminding him that U.S. support allowed the regime to stay in power for over six years.

After this long-winded speech, Greek prime minister Simitis took over but was more diplomatic. He tried to soften the atmosphere, and Clinton, in return, was very polite, very supportive. He also asked some of his Greek American delegation whom he brought with him, including me, to stand up. That evening was an experience I will remember all my life. The next day, the Greek American Chamber of Commerce invited President Clinton to speak to the members and invitees, so we gathered for breakfast at the intercontinental hotel where the president was staying. His first question to us was, "Why don't the Greek people like us?"

I was the first to respond, saying, "Mr. President, it is due to the United States having supported the military junta, and it would diffuse their anger if in your speech today you could give them some kind of an apology."

His response was quick: "I will do it."

In the hall, I was sitting in front when he did just that, and there was an unbelievable standing ovation afterward.

I learned through all of this how important it is for all of us to participate and become aware of issues and policies. We should strive to be good advisors to political leaders in our community and in our state and to our U.S. legislators and administrators.

George E. Danis

## CHAPTER THIRTEEN
# A PRESIDENTIAL CAMPAIGN UP CLOSE

WHILE PRESIDENT CARTER was about to lose to Reagan, Michael Dukakis convinced me that he could win a second term as governor of Massachusetts. He'd not been able to secure the nomination of the Democratic Party following his first term, so it was a long shot. But Michael made some convincing arguments about why he could—and should—run again. When I tested the idea with friends in the Greek community, they agreed. At a fundraiser at my home in Waltham, we raised $120,000 to help the Dukakis campaign get started.

Michael won, just as he said he would. I remained close to him throughout his second term as governor, even though I could not convince him to resist the urge to spend too much and tax too highly. I wanted him to be more of a centrist than he was willing to be, but I respected him for sticking to his position.

Integrity was never an issue with Michael. He would not let himself be persuaded to throw someone a favor just because they had power or influence. One time a Greek contact of mine asked me to help his friend secure a promotion at the Registry of Motor Vehicles. I told him it was doubtful but that I'd raise it with the governor and see what he suggested.

Michael's response was clear and simple: "George, he has to go through the process and meet with the RMV chairman. If the chairman thinks that he is qualified, he can be promoted."

The guy followed the advice, met with the chairman, but didn't get the promotion. My contact wasn't too happy, but I was delighted. Michael was totally committed to leveling the playing field, to working as hard as he could to ensure that all citizens had equal opportunity.

Michael's second term was a success. The tech boom was great for the state, and unemployment fell from 12 percent to 3. Taxes went down and income went up. The national press started referring to the "Massachusetts Miracle," and even though there was an attempt to split the Greek vote as the Republicans ran another local businessman against him in 1986, Michael's position was secure.

And so, in his third term as governor, I joined with him and a handful of close advisors at his house in Brookline. It was late November, and everyone in politics was talking about how to defeat Vice President George H.W. Bush in the next year's election. Senator Gary Hart of Colorado was the front runner among Democrats and was the presumptive nominee. He and Michael were politically compatible, and Hart represented the western part of the country well, but he was weak in the east. So our topic was simple: Should

Governor Dukakis make a presidential run with a view of becoming vice president of the United States?

The answer was a unanimous yes.

We set the wheels in motion by trying to figure out whether we would be able to raise the required levels of funding to mount a bid—a figure somewhere in the region of $18.5 million. I was part of the finance committee and traveled the country, paying particular attention to those cities like New York, Chicago, Philadelphia, and the state of California, which had large Greek populations. The reaction was overwhelmingly positive, and by the spring of 1987, we reached our target.

With the first test passed, Michael, in March of 1987, walked down from the governor's office to Boston Common on a snowy day and announced his candidacy, before spending the rest of the day giving the same speech in Atlanta and finally in Iowa. From that moment on, the lives of all of us working at the heart of the campaign were taken over completely.

I spent much of the rest of 1987 traveling. Weekdays I'd spend at home or wherever I needed to be for the business, while weekends were nearly all spent in Iowa, preparing for the first primary. I was exhausted on those weekends, but often I'd be woken up by a phone call at 5:30 a.m. Michael would be inviting me for a run, and it was impossible to say no.

While Michael had me beat in terms of fitness, I knew I could teach him a thing or two about how to dress right.

He was not a fan of expensive suits, and while I respected his economic frugality, I felt like he needed help to present a better image. I knew him well enough to understand that a direct assault would get me nowhere, so I took the side route.

"I'm just thinking," I said to Michael's wife, Kitty, one day as we stood at one of the Iowa debates, watching Michael glad-hand a room full of people. He was looking particularly low-grade that day, with his poorly cut suit showing clear signs of age. "Do you think maybe he needs some new suits?"

She smiled the smile of a woman who had tried—and failed—to tackle that particular problem many times. "If you can convince him, I'd be really grateful."

I arranged for Kitty to get me one of Michael's suits, which I then took with me a few days later to a clothing retailer, Eastern Clothing. The owner, John, was a friend from back in Watertown, where we had worked together on many civic projects. He took the measurements from the old suit, and we then picked out three new suits, along with matching shirts and ties.

When Michael saw them next weekend, he asked two questions.

"How much did these cost? And is this anything to do with George?"

He insisted that he pay, and even though I told him that I had spent about $375, he wouldn't believe me. He sent me a check for $600. It was classic Michael: honest, unimpressed by the trappings of power, full of integrity. He didn't care at all whether people thought badly of how he dressed, and he was always anxious to treat people with generosity. He cared very little about his own needs but was determined to use all of his energy to make sure that the people he served had what they needed.

The campaign was going as well as we hoped it would, until that summer. That's when the wheels came off the campaign—but not ours. There were rumors that Gary Hart had been having an affair, and in an interview with the *New York Times* he denied it with the words, "Follow me around. I don't care. I'm serious. If anybody wants to put a tail on me, go ahead. They'll be very bored."

Well, two reporters from the *Miami Herald* had been doing just that. First, they identified a young woman leaving Hart's Washington, D.C., townhouse as a model named Donna Rice. Then they photographed her sitting on Hart's knee on a boat named *Monkey Business*. Hart tried to fight his way out of the scandal and put the blame on the press, but the damage was done. Hart's integrity was shot through, and his bid to secure the nomination was dead in the water. Suddenly, Michael wasn't looking to squeeze his way onto the ticket as vice president anymore: he was a viable contender for the nomination itself.

We had serious momentum behind us, and early in the fall we were getting ready to host a large fundraiser at the World Trade Center in Boston. People were coming in from all over the country, a lot of them Greeks, and many of them cochairs of finance committees. It was going to be like a Greek wedding, with envelopes bearing checks handed over by smiling well-wishers. We were hoping to raise over $2 million. It was going to be a huge moment for the campaign, one that would show the country that Michael was capable of really connecting with people.

It was going to be the focus of the press for a while at least, but—as always seems to be the case in politics—things don't always go as planned. During the run up to the fundraiser, the press chose instead to focus on a story that did us no favors with voters at all.

The problem was a certain Senator Joe Biden from Delaware. He was hoping for the nomination, too, and was still in the running. Back in August, Senator Biden gave a speech at the Iowa State Fair in which he appeared to have plagiarized a section from a speech given earlier that year by the leader of the British Labor Party, Neil Kinnock. Later, it became clear that Senator Biden had given the speech before and always credited Kinnock. But in Iowa, he used the words as if they were his own, and an attack video emerged exposing the plagiarism. It was a powerful ad and forced Senator Biden to withdraw.

Theft aside, Senator Biden was an effective speaker. He was politically moderate and had already amassed a lot of legislative experience. In many ways he looked like the candidate that the Dukakis campaign was most worried about. So when the attack video emerged—a few days before our epic fundraiser—most people assumed that we were the ones behind it.

We denied it, but the rumors persisted. Soon the story of

our fundraising triumph was a distant memory. All people wanted to talk about was whether we had been the ones to sink low and torpedo the senator's campaign. We carried on denying it, but the rumors refused to die. Soon, the press even had names, accusing the campaign manager, John Sasso, and political director, Paul Tully, of being behind the ad.

The day of the fundraiser I was at a lunch with Michael. He asked me to travel back with him to the statehouse, and as we were sitting in the back of the car, he took me by surprise.

"Tomorrow we have to announce that John Sasso will no longer be part of our campaign."

I didn't know what to say. I was stunned, concerned, and couldn't believe that this was happening on the day of our big event. I also wasn't sure that firing John would work, but Michael had already made up his mind, and I knew that the best thing to do was to focus on finding a replacement.

The fundraiser went well—so well that we even exceeded our $2 million target—but the press wasn't interested. Even in the campaign there was no time to sit back and relax: now we had to find a new campaign manager.

Michael asked a few of us for names. I strongly recommended Bob Strauss, who was one of the real heavyweights in the Democratic Party. He spent five years as chairman of the Democratic National Committee and then chaired Jimmy Carter's successful presidential run. He was connected, charismatic, and—best of all—he had already donated to Michael's campaign and sent me a note offering to help. I couldn't think of anyone better than Bob to get us out of our mess. Even the news of bringing him on board would be enough to jolt the news cycle away from the attack ad.

Michael didn't agree. Though I pleaded with him to reconsider, he felt that Bob was just too conservative in his politics and that the two of them would not be able to work together. Maybe he was right, and maybe I was wrong about Bob being able to turn us around. We'll never know, but what is clear is that the new campaign chairman that Michael brought in took us in a new direction that ultimately proved to be even more costly to us.

The new guy was Paul Brountas, an old friend of Michael's from when they were at Harvard Law School together. Michael also brought in a young Harvard professor of criminal law named Susan Estrich as national campaign manager. Although Susan had some experience working as policy advisor to Ted Kennedy and Walter Mondale, she had little real experience with running a campaign, not that this bothered Michael: he was convinced that she had all the necessary skills.

By the time February 1988 came around and the Iowa caucuses loomed, the press had moved on from the attack ad, and we were able to focus on the primaries. Michael came in third in Iowa, with 22 percent. Next came New Hampshire a week later, which Michael won. Super Tuesday was the next big event in early March, with seventeen primaries and five caucuses all held on the same day. I was sent to Tampa because of the significant Greek community there, and after a lot of hard work, we won that primary too. We identified volunteers from all over the community, who we used to call on Democrats from our voting lists and other sources. It was an interesting experience for me but a lot of hard work. The Greek community was committed, including several restaurant owners who went beyond their civic responsibilities and roasted lamb to feed the volunteers. When the polls closed, everyone had a lot of fun, especially when the Greek live music and dancing started up. It all paid off in the end, as we won Florida as well as Wyoming, Hawaii, Idaho, Maryland, Massachusetts, Rhode Island, Texas, Washington, and American Samoa—making us the clear victors of Super Tuesday.

After that it was on to New York for the April 19 primary. One of our big competitors there was Al Gore. His ad campaign targeted Michael, accusing him of being too liberal. Gore was the first person to mention Willie Horton, a convicted murderer who had been sentenced to life imprisonment in Massachusetts and released from jail for the weekend under a law signed into effect by one of Michael's predecessors as governor. Willie Horton did not return to jail when he was supposed to and went on to rape a woman. Michael supported the program under which Willie Horton had been released and even vetoed a bill that would have prohibited first-degree murderers like Willie Horton from accessing the program.

While Al Gore did not mention Willie Horton by name, he pressed the bruise by discussing the weekend-pass program. It backfired for him, and after a poor showing in New

York, he soon dropped out. But Willie Horton would come back and haunt us later.

---

"So if we win…who does what?"

The question stopped me in my tracks. We were flying home to Boston after the New York primary, and the conversation took an unexpected turn. As Michael and I talked about possible names for cabinet positions, it was clear that we were a lot less prepared than we needed to be. We had spent so long aiming for VP, then got caught up in the dog fight to secure the nomination, that we never seriously mapped out our plan for what would happen if we won. But with Gore, Biden, and Hart all out, it was looking like the nomination was Michael's to win.

For a boy like me who had grown up barefoot and afraid of Nazis, this was a dizzying turn of events. Only in America could someone come from so far away and find themselves playing an important role in deciding who might be its next leaders. Opportunity thrives in America like nowhere else on Earth. The ancient Greeks believed that the three Fates determined not only how long a person would live but also what his lot in life would be and that nothing could change that. I suppose that fate or luck can play a role in our destiny, but when I think about my own life, I am convinced that it was shaped by my early goals and ambitions. I was able to travel from poverty in Mili to wealth and influence in America not primarily because I was lucky, but because I was determined. If you don't give up, the possibilities just keep on coming.

Despite the successes up to that point and the loss of so many other candidates, we still didn't have the primary locked up. There was one other candidate in the race whose star had continued to rise: Jesse Jackson. He won eleven primaries and caucuses, scored 20 percent of the vote, and felt that he had a real shot at vice president. Since we knew that we'd need to keep Jackson on our side if we were to have any hope of winning the support of the Black community, Michael invited him and his wife to join him and Kitty at the Fourth of July Boston Pops concert and fireworks display.

The evening started with dinner at Michael's house: a New England classic of creamy clam chowder and salmon poached in milk. Unfortunately, Jackson had a milk allergy and couldn't eat any of it. He asked for some fried chicken instead, so we scrambled around to find Kentucky Fried Chicken for our guest, but it wasn't a great start to their relationship.

The primary campaign finally ended before the Democratic National Convention in July. Despite having won the nomination, Michael was not well known nationally, so it was time to bring in some reinforcements. What we needed was a keynote speaker who had a strong reputation and who would come out and swing for Michael. There was only one name: Senator Ted Kennedy.

Senator Kennedy and I had become friends over the years, and I had often visited him at his home in Arlington,

Virginia, or in Hyannis Port on Cape Cod. Whenever he came to Boston, he would call me and meet for a meal. One morning, the senator and his wife, Vicky, joined me at the Ritz Carlton for breakfast. He looked at me and said, "I am mad at you."

"Why, Senator?"

"You are not a registered Democrat."

"Yes," I said. "I am an American."

He looked vaguely offended. "Well, what the hell do you think I am?"

"You chose to be a senator of a political party aligned with your ideology. I choose to be an independent citizen so I can choose who will do a good job for my country. I chose to support you because your policies are close to my expectations of a more level playing field for our citizens."

He thought a while. "You are right. That sounds like a Greek independent, free mind."

---

Many times, when the senator wanted to test some ideas out, he'd include me in a group of half a dozen people whom he trusted to discuss things with. But while Ted and I were close, the relationship between him and Michael was less warm. Michael and the senator went way back, and their history in Boston politics hadn't always been harmonious. The Irish and Greek communities had not always gelled in the city, and some of that mistrust spilled over into politics. Still, it was decided that Senator Kennedy was the only man for the job, and—given my close relationship with him—I was asked to make the approach.

I knew that Senator Kennedy would say yes, and I knew, too, that he would be able to deliver when he gave his speech to the conference. But so, too, did Jesse Jackson. The night before the nominating speech, Jackson took to the stage and captivated the hall. He talked about his rise from poverty and his fight for racial equality, and the crowd was hooked. They gave him eighteen standing ovations during the course of the speech, and overnight Jackson became the focus of the whole event.

So the next night we had a job to do. We needed to get the focus back on Michael, to convince the country that this was the man they wanted to serve as their president. The nominating speaker was none other than the governor of Arkansas, William Jefferson Clinton. He was a rising star within the party, and he and Michael had become friends through the National Governors Association. They were kindred spirits—new liberal pragmatists who believed in education and economics. Even better, Clinton was a great orator. If anybody was going to bring the focus back to Michael, it was Bill Clinton.

He failed.

The speech started later in the evening than was planned, which wasn't a good start. It was also thirty-three minutes, twice as long as expected. And it was dull. Clinton lost the crowd a few minutes in, and he never got them back. People were talking among themselves, and eventually the networks cut away from him altogether. It was a disaster, and the only line that generated any applause was when Clinton announced, "In closing…"

I was sitting in the front row next to Governor Clinton. When he returned to his seat, he looked defeated and more than a little annoyed about the whole thing. We'd put too much on him, and he knew it.

"You guys really screwed me there," he said.

"No," I replied, scrambling for the right words to say. "No. It wasn't meant to be that way. Really it wasn't."

Years later at the New York democratic convention in '92, when he made his acceptance speech as the presidential nominee, Governor Clinton started his speech by calling himself the "Comeback Kid." He'd already learned the value of good public relations skills.

---

The question of who we should select as running mate was another call that didn't go quite as well as it could have. A few of us argued hard for Al Gore, the young, energetic Southerner who had campaigned with so much energy. Even better, he knew about fundraising too. In my mind he was far and away the best choice. But Michael wanted nothing to do with Al Gore. The whole Willie Horton incident still stung, and there was no way on earth that Michael would have considered sharing the ticket with him. We had several meetings with Michael on selecting Al Gore to be VP, but we were not able to convince Michael to change his mind.

Michael's preference was Senator Lloyd Bentsen from Texas. Michael hoped that with a Texan at his side, he would have a shot at the state. But with his Republican opponent named as George H.W. Bush—a man who had made his home in West Texas since the war—there was no way that Michael could ever hope to win in the Lone Star State.

Things continued to deteriorate as Jesse Jackson started to press his case for being on the ticket as VP candidate. After all, he'd finished second in the race for the nomination, and he was the only candidate who could reach the Black community. He felt like he deserved to be selected. Though Michael was still unsure and was leaning toward Senator Bentsen, Michael and Jesse Jackson communicated, and Michael gave his assurance that Jackson would be told of his decision before it went public.

Unfortunately, that's not how it happened.

Michael decided that Bentsen was the best choice and decided to act immediately. He spoke to the senator early one morning around 6:30 a.m. and offered him the slot on the ticket. Bentsen said yes right away, and Michael decided to travel to his Boston statehouse office before telling anyone else. So it was 8:20 a.m. by the time he picked up the phone to tell Jesse Jackson that he was not his choice of running mate. This was before cell phones, and Jackson was not at home—he was on his way to the airport to fly to Washington. As a further twist, Jackson had told Michael's campaign the day before that he was leaving for the airport at 8 a.m. sharp, reminding them that he did not want to read about the decision in the press before hearing from Michael himself.

Of course, Jackson learned of the Bentsen selection from a reporter, and the narrative was set that Michael was never really seriously considering Jackson for vice president and he'd only been toying with him to keep Michael out of trouble. Many of Jackson's supporters felt snubbed and disrespected. It would be hard to blame them for it.

In time Jackson's anger eased, and he toured the country making speeches for Michael, but the damage was done. The Black community never really developed any enthusiasm for Michael, which only added to the damage that was weakening the campaign. When the Republicans seized on the Willie Horton incident that Al Gore first used, the story received a lot of coverage. The Republicans didn't hold back like Gore did but utilized the attack as much as possible. They spread a lot of untruths about a Dukakis presidency opening the prison doors to rapists and murderers, which terrified plenty of would-be Democrat voters.

Perhaps the greatest damage was caused by blunders from within. During a debate, Michael was asked whether he would favor the death penalty if his wife, Kitty, was raped and murdered. It was a ridiculous question that Michael should have dealt with easily, but instead he launched into a dispassionate, unemotional monologue, making him appear kind of odd in the eyes of many potential voters.

Then there was the awkward photo op of Michael riding in an Abrams tank, smiling as if he were appearing on *The Muppet Show*. By that point, the campaign was sunk. It was such a shame, not just for me personally but for the country at large. Michael was, and still is, an honorable, good man. He had the integrity and intellect to serve our country well, but issues of communication and campaigning prevented the voters from seeing enough of those great qualities to give him a chance. As the campaign entered its dying days, the mood was somber. The prospect of victory was long gone. The only question facing us was whether there was any chance of salvaging some pride and scoring a few symbolically significant wins.

George H.W. Bush won in a landslide.

## CHAPTER FOURTEEN
# BACK TO BUSINESS

THROUGHOUT THE CAMPAIGN I was somehow able to keep DAMCO and Fastener Supply running well and making a profit, and I was grateful for the choices I had made early on to ensure that my businesses could run without me. But even before Michael's bid for the presidency died, I was feeling the pull of business again. Things were just beginning to change in the industry, and I wanted to be a part of it.

For one thing, as the company continued to flourish and grow, I needed additional space. I negotiated a lease with my abutting neighbor and started to move some machines and business into the new building.

I also rented some of the upper floors of my building to my friend Peter, who was also Greek and founded Boston Scientific. This turned out to be a wise move, since I sold the building to Peter for $5.5 million in 1989.

The changes within the world of manufacturing in those days were colossal. The computer industry was no longer making room-sized machines but had evolved to produce far smaller units that would fit under or on top of a desk. This promoted a move away from metal housing and cabinets to small, complicated plastic parts. With DAMCO specializing in metal fabrication and Fastener Supply distributing metal parts, I needed to keep pace with the changes.

I considered the idea of starting a plastics company from the bottom up, but the speed of change in the industry made that idea redundant. I needed to be able to offer plastic computer casings and internal parts *now*, not in a year or two once I'd learned everything I needed to know about the industry and built the appropriate infrastructure. So I went looking for an established plastics company that I could buy and eventually found one in Connecticut that was looking for an investor.

I visited the company and listened as the broker outlined the pitch: they were valuing the company at $1 million and were willing to sell me 40 percent. I studied the paperwork, scrutinizing it just as I had when Fastener Supply was in trouble or DAMCO needed support. I saw some familiar things—uncollected debts, poor pricing, a lack of liquidity required to keep things running smoothly—and reached the conclusion that their estimate of the company's worth was about ten times higher than it ought to be.

I told the company's president and the broker that I wasn't interested in investing, as I felt that the company was wildly overvalued. They acted surprised, but something told me that they knew it too.

"Listen," I said, feeling compassionate for the place they were in. "I think there are a few things you can do to help get yourself out of this mess. I'd be happy to share my thoughts if you wanted to hear them?"

The broker wasn't interested, but the president was receptive, so I outlined a few simple steps: collect all receivables in a timelier manner, renegotiate the interest on the debts the company was carrying, and get the suppliers to agree to more favorable terms.

"That can't be done," said the president.

"Anything can be done," I said. "You just need to make your case in a clear enough manner."

It wasn't a long conversation, and I had no idea whether the president was taking me seriously or trying to figure out if I was bluffing (I wasn't). As we were wrapping up and I was preparing to leave, the production manager asked me, "How do you know so much about our business?"

"I don't," I said, pointing to the pile of statements on the desk between us. "But your paperwork tells me everything."

A few months later the production manager called me up. They had tried to make the changes, but things didn't work out the way he'd hoped. He was closing the business. I was genuinely sad for them, since I was honest when I'd told him that he had a chance of turning things around. To close down a company that you've put so much energy and effort into for so many years isn't easy. But any sorrow I felt for the guy was brief. At last he had a clear and realistic view of what the company was really worth. He stopped listening to what the greedy broker was telling him and was finally prepared to accept a fair and reasonable price for it.

I bought it for $85,000.

I hired their production manager, Richard McKinney. He was an expert in plastic injection molding, and he told me that he had gone home and told his wife that this young guy with a heavy accent knew more about our company than the president.

"What should we name the company?" he asked me.

"What do we make?" I asked.

The answer was obvious. We called the company Plastic Molding Manufacturing and moved the three plastic molding machines into the premises in Moosup, Connecticut.

Finally, we were in the plastic injection molding business. We had a total of fifteen machines and an okay building in Connecticut. It was time to start introducing ourselves as a plastic molding manufacturing company.

Our first customer was Motorola, and from then on, many others followed, and the business grew fast. My plan was to eventually move Plastic Molding Manufacturing closer to DAMCO—or perhaps even within the same building. Richard was willing to travel to Massachusetts, but the space at DAMCO was already tight, and with the new equipment, we already outgrew our premises and desperately needed more space. I went back to my old routine of driving around the local streets, scouring the area for a possible new home.

I found it in Reading, Massachusetts, in a former tire factory set on eighteen acres. The site had four hundred thousand square feet of space, though the buildings were divided up and scattered across the land. I took a few trips to visit it and spent many hours staring at the buildings and the space between them, trying to let my imagination conjure up a plan that would work. It wasn't easy to see the potential clearly, but my gut told me that this was the right place for us.

Many of my staff, on the other hand, disagreed. Right from the start I'd taken them along with me, when I was still wondering how I could configure the site, and I was genuinely interested in their opinions. Yet most of them couldn't see it. They'd stare, wide-eyed, at the giant oil tanks and ugly-looking boiler houses and struggle to see anything else.

"We'll fix it," I told them.

"How?" they'd ask.

I'd try to explain, but the truth was that I wasn't completely clear myself. All I knew for sure was that this giant, sprawling, ugly site had potential. And potential was all that I really needed.

After several weeks of visiting and staring and wondering out loud, I acquired the site for $4.5 million. I then spent at least that much over the following year to reconfigure it and demolish some of the small buildings—an interesting process, as there were small buildings inside of other buildings. We also took down the oil tank and repaved the thousand parking spaces. I used reserves to pay for everything, and it felt like the second-most significant investment I'd made up to then. So when the work was finally complete and the place was ready to be occupied, I was excited to move in.

Fastener Supply and DAMCO had never shared the same location, but Reading gave us the opportunity to change that.

We also brought up the rest of the plastic injection molding equipment from the company I'd bought in Connecticut and moved everything in together to our new four-hundred-thousand-square-foot home.

We occupied only about half the space, but that didn't bother me at all. I saw it as a great opportunity and set myself the task of using the rest as efficiently as possible. I rented a little under one hundred thousand square feet to a company that was handling deliveries and logistics for other businesses, then some more space to a removals company. Feeling good, I continued searching for another business to take on the rest.

I found my answer in a business called Frugal Fannie's. I'd never heard of it before, but the more I discovered, the more I liked it. They acted like a wholesaler for low-cost overruns of women's apparel and had over one hundred thousand customers. But the genius part of it was that they were only ever open on Friday afternoons, weekends, and holidays—all times when our operation was pretty much shut. That meant they could have full use of the parking lot without causing our businesses any trouble.

The site no longer felt so empty, but it didn't take long for the real benefit of the three leases to be felt. The rental income was significant and allowed me to do everything I wanted. Top of my list was ensuring that my children's education was the very best it could be.

The girls were growing up fast. Stella had already started at Regis College in Waltham and then transferred to Boston University. She also worked on the fundraising team for the Dukakis presidential campaign and met a young man whom she married in 1989. Barbara, Marina, and Jennifer all attended private school—Dana Hall in Wellesley—and continued on to college after that. Barbara went to Brown, then got her PhD from the University of Denver. Marina was president of her class for her junior and senior years at Dana Hall, and I was able to invite Senator Kennedy to speak to the college for Constitution Week on her behalf. She then went to Skidmore in upstate New York, before going to the University of Pennsylvania and getting her master's in education. Jennifer went to Hampshire College in Massachusetts, and then to the University of Denver, where she got a master's in psychology. To say I am proud of them all is an understatement.

---

The cash cow of my Watertown and Reading properties, along with the success of each of the individual businesses, allowed me to explore other business opportunities. In 1987 I acquired a ten-acre lot on Route One in Lynnfield—an ideal place to build some office buildings. Strangely, the lot already had a restaurant on it, and it was one of the strangest locations I had ever seen: a 120-foot, bright-red schooner placed in the middle of a parking lot that had been converted to a very well-known, much-loved restaurant that was able to accommodate six hundred diners. My plan was to tear it down as soon as possible, but the restaurant was a local landmark and the sale was conditional on it continuing to operate for a period of time. So more than two decades after

I was cooking eggs and burgers in Mr. Contos's diner, I found myself back in the restaurant business.

I bought the place in November and chose not to mess with anything for a while but let the management keep doing what they were doing. The Ship served classic steak and seafood, including lobsters and a colossal three-and-a-half-pound steak called The Bostonian. That first Thanksgiving they had over 2,200 reservations, and it quickly became clear to me that the place had a lot of potential, and not just to make money, either.

Each year at Thanksgiving, I would spend the day running around, hosting the Watertown local senior citizens at The Ship. I relished the opportunity to see so many people enjoy a free meal. It was like being back in Greece, listening to the sound of a crowd of happy diners all enjoying each other's company.

I ran the restaurant for a few years but soon discovered an uncomfortable truth: every time I visited the place, I felt sick. It wasn't down to the quality of the food or service. It was me: I was a perfectionist. Every time I visited, I found something that I felt sure we could improve upon. And in a restaurant of that size, there was a lot of potential for improvement.

When the time was right, I redesigned The Ship's internal layout. I kept the restaurant upstairs—though reduced its capacity to 150 diners—and converted the lower deck to a retail space. These were the days of Yankee Candle, candy stores, and other boutiques, and a quirky location like The Ship made a perfect home. It was another big success.

George E. Danis

Things improved further when the owner of a retail store, The Christmas Tree Shops from Cape Cod, asked if we could partner up and build a store on the site. I liked the idea a lot, and after securing the financing, went ahead and built a wonderful facility right there by The Ship. It was the first Christmas Tree Shops of its kind away from the Cape, and people came all the way from New England to buy their products and home decorations. Between the retail space, the restaurant, and my share of the profits of the wildly successful Christmas Tree Shops venture, business was thriving like never before.

---

As I looked around for other projects to invest in, my eyes settled on one new venture in particular. Only, it wasn't a location or an existing business. It was a person: George, the son of my eldest brother, Evangelis.

My nephew and I had always been close. He came to the United States from Greece in 1976 and did his undergraduate at Boston University before going on to the University of Connecticut, where he first earned a PhD in biochemistry and then an MBA. He worked for Pfizer and was a wonderful young man. I was pleased to help him throughout his studies, and as he grew up, he became a true friend, a trusted confidant, and a wise advisor. If there was anyone on the planet that I wanted to start a business with, it was George.

His unique skills and training led us in a clear direction: cosmetics. We started in Greece, working with dermatologists there and importing a range of creams, colognes, and soaps from the United States and from an English supplier. It became very successful, and soon we wanted to expand. We sourced new products from Italy and started funding dermatologists in Greece, sponsoring conventions and further research. It was an expensive business to be in, with high advertising costs, but it was rewarding to be able to work with George. We even managed to persuade my brother Alexandros to join the company and gave him the task of finding new suppliers in Greece as well as promoting and distributing the product.

The ultimate test of the business was whether we could make it work in America. We negotiated with an American company out of New Jersey to distribute over here and later acquired an Italian company that already had a business in New York. New doors opened up, and we were able to get into spas all over the country. Suddenly, our products were available everywhere from Fifth Avenue all the way to California and Florida at the Doral Country Club and the famous Terme Di Saturnia spa. It was an exciting time, but eventually the energy started to leak from it. Because it was a family-run business, I could not extricate myself from the day-to-day affairs as I had with my manufacturing companies. I needed to be involved, to put in the hours just like George and Alexandros were expected to do. That meant weekly trips to New York and beyond—time that I knew I could be spending profitably elsewhere. Between this, the rising costs of advertising, and the fact that working with my younger brother Alexandros was a lot more complicated than I assumed it would be, we eventually sold the business to a company in Greece.

This whole period of my life working in the cosmetics industry was full of opportunities to learn valuable lessons. My previous experience in manufacturing meant I was used to dealing largely with businesses or the industry itself. All I needed to do was sell to a dozen purchasing managers, and I could have a viable customer base. Cosmetics were different. I found myself dealing directly with consumers—the spas and boutiques that would stock our products. Instead of persuading a handful of people to place orders with us worth millions, I had to convince millions of customers to spend just a few dollars. The potential rewards were great, but the costs required to reach that many people were vast.

I was aware of this before George and I started the business, but I wasn't fully knowledgeable about the lengths to which I would have to go—the relentless travel, the expensive promotion and PR—in order to build a successful cosmetics business. It taught me to be more diligent in the future before starting a new venture, but I do not regret the time or money spent. I had a lot of fun working with George, and I was able to get a glimpse into the world of retail and try my hand at promotion. I also met thousands of people in the business who were charming and wonderful company. It allowed me to relax a little and reveal a part of myself that I didn't often show.

One winter, just after Christmas, I was down in Florida. I had rented a condo for the winter and would spend most of the week in Boston, then hurry back to the winter sun on weekends. I'd been working with a local resort in Fort Lauderdale—the Bonaventure resort—and the spa manager became a good customer.

Our big customer at the Doral invited me to join them for dinner at New Year's. There were going to be some other guests and managers of the spa there—a dozen in total—and the manager offered me a complimentary room. It was 1990, and the nightly room rate was somewhere around $650. I didn't wait to be asked twice.

I turned up in the afternoon and booked myself in for a massage. The masseuse had a big, beautiful bouquet of roses on display, and I couldn't help but compliment her on them.

"Thanks," she said. "They're a gift from my husband."

"Well, congratulations. You clearly picked a good man there."

The massage was excellent, and afterward I went back to my room to get ready for the evening meal. It struck me that if there were going to be managers with their wives at the dinner, this was a chance for me to show off and maybe do more business there too. I figured I probably ought to be prepared to make a good impression. I thought back to the roses and put in a call to a local florist, asking if they could send over a big bouquet.

"Sure. I can get it to you by January 3."

I called a few more, but nobody could help me on such short notice. So I went to plan B and called the masseuse.

"I need your help," I told her. "I need to borrow your roses. I'll send you a replacement in a couple of days."

She smiled and handed the flowers over. "You don't need to replace them. Please, have them."

I was taken aback by her kindness and insisted that I would replace them as promised.

I went back to my room and placed an order with the florist, then called up the concierge and asked for their help too. I had them take the bouquet and prepare a dozen individual red roses with some nice foliage.

But that wasn't enough for me, so I went out looking for a supermarket to purchase a cake. Finally, I found one, and even though it was late, I begged them to cut the cake in twelve pieces and change dollars to coins and place a coin under each piece of the cake. I took it back to the hotel dining room and gave it to the maître d' to put in the refrigerator until the end of our dinner. It was time to go fully Greek.

Later that evening, when the main course was over and midnight was approaching, I handed each of the ladies a single red rose. Then I asked the waiters to bring in the cake, which had been sliced up and served onto individual plates.

"We have a New Year's tradition in Greece," I said. "We take a single coin and bury it in a cake. The person who gets the coin is considered very lucky for the rest of the year. But I don't wish just one of you to be lucky; I want you all to have a wonderful 1991. So each of you has a coin in there. Go carefully, okay?"

It was the kind of thing I would never have done at a meeting of executives from AT&T, IBM, or Data General, and if I'd pulled a stunt like that on the campaign trail, I would have been laughed out of the room and sent home on the next available flight. But the cosmetics industry was different. It was fun, it didn't take itself too seriously, and a little bit of exhibitionism didn't do you any harm at all. It was a world where the bolder you were, the better. For too long I'd buried that part of me. It was good to know that it still existed.

———————

There were other lessons that I learned from that period as well, especially about the dangers of growth. I was well prepared to handle the growth that followed our move to Reading and the purchase of the lot with The Ship restaurant. I had big renovations but kept my plans relatively modest and was always careful to keep the levels of debt as low as possible. If I had taken a different path and tried to leverage all that liquidity the properties were generating and used it to service the maximum levels of borrowing, I would have overextended myself. That would have left me stretched thin and vulnerable to the slightest downturn in the market.

I have seen too many businesses take this path, and for many the end result is often bankruptcy. It happened more than once to Donald Trump. Even Orange County in California filed for Chapter 9 in 1994. Whether it's an individual, a corporation, or a county, the result of overextending yourself financially is always the same: the debtors pay the price.

———————

George E. Danis

Our country, like so many others in the developed world, appears to be addicted to borrowing. We keep on adding to our debts, doing things that we really can't afford, and all the time we're feeding up a catastrophe in waiting. At some point it's going to all come crashing down, and it will be the next generation that plays the role of debtor.

---

So many people have helped me on my business journey, but I would particularly like to thank three key individuals, all of whom served as my chief of staff. These special people were extraordinary team members and sources of great support throughout some of my most challenging times.

My first attempt to find a chief of staff did not start well. We had four plants at that time, and I had also just started CosMed LLC, the cosmetics company, with offices in the United States, Italy, France, and Greece. We also did some food exports from the United States, Canada, and Thailand, shipping them to Greece, and we were importing Cavino wine from Greece to the United States. We marketed the wine all over New England, including the New Hampshire state liquor stores. I desperately needed a chief of staff, but after many unsuccessful interviews, I was feeling disappointed.

Then one day I walked out to our Fastener Supply operation office, where a saleslady called Jane Argento was working. I had seen Jane a few times before, and she was always very appreciative about working with us and loyal to our business. She was also very understanding of my deficiencies in the English language. She took on the chief of staff job, and we became a good team, working together for over twenty-five years until Jane decided to retire. She was my confidant, my advisor, part of the family, and, in many ways, like a sister to me. I will always appreciate all she did for me and my family, especially during my separation and divorce from Kathy.

When Jane retired, I invited her and her husband, Joe, to Greece for two weeks. We traveled around from one end of the country to the other, including the islands and my hometown. The three of us together had a lot of fun.

Jane helped find her replacement and recommended someone she had interviewed called Jeannie. Jane was out of the office on the day Jeannie came in to meet me, and things were so hectic that day that Jeannie ended up waiting thirty minutes on her own in the conference room. When I finally joined her, I apologized for being late. She accepted my apology with a smile but commented that I definitely needed someone to help me get organized. We talked for over an hour, and Jeannie told me about her previous job as chief of staff to a governor in a New England state. I was sold, and after she negotiated herself an improved compensation package, she came on board.

Jeannie and I worked together very well for over eight years. She helped a lot with the advertising and promotion of our CosMed business, and we set up a continuous improvement quarterly meeting with over forty line managers from all the businesses that I was running. Jeannie was an extraordinary individual with a lot of patience and experience in the business world, including the protocol of the chief of staff, and I enjoyed and cherished her teamwork and confidentiality. Unfortunately for me, her husband started his own business as an environmental engineer, and when he needed her assistance, Jeannie resigned.

It was hard to replace both Jane and Jeannie. It took me a year, and three or four people who didn't work out, to finally find Jody Heyward, who is still with me now, twenty years after she started. I must say that I'm lucky to have found Jody as my third chief of staff in my business world, and in fact, now we are more active than ever before. Jody has been a savior in every way, especially when it comes to today's technologies, which move faster than I am able to keep up with.

It has been exciting to have three extraordinary, exceptional team members helping me. They have been a tremendous assistance in my career, and if I could have talked to my mother about them, she would have been unsurprised. "Their names begin with J—it is a good omen, for it is the same letter as 'Jesus.'"

## CHAPTER FIFTEEN
# THE CURTAIN FALLS

IN THE DYING WEEKS OF THE 1980s, two Russian words became commonplace in the English language: *glasnost* and *perestroika*. The Cold War had been going on for decades, and after so much mistrust, misinformation, and the continual threat of mutually assured destruction, it was a little strange to hear these foreign words on the tongues of politicians, the media, and everyday people. But in the space of a few short years, the world had begun to change. Relations between the United States and the Soviet Union were improving. Finally, the long winter was coming to an end.

The man responsible for so much of this change—as well as for popularizing both words—was Mikhail Gorbachev, general secretary of the Communist Party of the Soviet Union. He was the one who called for *glasnost*, a policy of openness after decades of secrecy. He was the one who sold the idea of *perestroika*, the political movement committed to reconstruction. Gorbachev was a unique man with both the potential and the courage to change the course of history. The eyes of the world were upon him.

Gorbachev did not stay in power for long once the Soviet Union collapsed, but he remained committed to the cause of democracy in Russia and peace in the world. When I heard that he was planning a two-week tour of the United States in the early summer of 1992—and that he had been invited to Boston by Senator Kennedy—I was both intrigued and excited about the chance to hear him speak.

The event was held at the Kennedy Library, toward the end of Gorbachev's tour of the country. Right from the start it was clear that it was going to be a special evening. I had an invitation to join the senator, and at the event the Kennedy family was well represented, including a rare public appearance from President Kennedy's widow, Jacqueline Kennedy Onassis.

Interest in the event was high. For the previous two weeks of his tour, Gorbachev had spoken all over the country, raising money for a new foundation he was launching in both Moscow and San Francisco. Rumor had it that he had raised over $2 million. It was a lot of money for a man to raise but just an insignificant fraction of the amount that his predecessors—and the leaders that followed—would spend on arms each year. Peace, it seemed to me at the time, didn't always have to come with a high price tag.

Gorbachev himself was inspiring. "Today," he announced, "we are all acutely aware that it would be criminal to miss the chance to carry through on the historic shifts that have been maturing for so long, and that we vitally need a policy worthy of the scientific and technical achievements of the times and of the new discoveries promised in the century to come."

But he also had a warning: the "manifestations of chaos, collapse, and loss of control" demanded that we "seek the paths to an intelligent and necessarily democratic organization to our common abode."

Thirty years later, with Putin waging war on Ukraine, violating human rights, and committing war crimes, Gorbachev's words have even greater resonance. The chance to bring reform was missed. The chaos, collapse, and loss of control won.

---

I was not the only one who was impressed by Gorbachev on his visit to the United States. A friend of mine, another George, decided to start the Gorbachev Foundation of North America in 1997. George was a retired Greek American entrepreneur and philanthropist, and he persuaded several of us to join him and set up the foundation at Northeastern University. The Gorbachev Foundation of North America's mission was clear: we wanted to "contribute to the strengthening and spread of democracy and economic liberalization through a program of advocacy, research, and education." We wanted to support peace initiatives all over the world and do what we could to empower Gorbachev and his ideals. Given that he had been replaced as Russia's president first by the alcoholic Boris Yeltsin, then by the despot Vladimir Putin, we figured he needed all the help he could get.

I was able to hear Gorbachev speak many times over the years and was even lucky enough to sit and eat with him on several occasions. There, around a table with a dozen or so others, I got to see the man up close, to study him a little. What I saw left me even more impressed than when I first heard him at the Kennedy Library. He was intelligent, well-informed, and fully committed to the ideals of democracy.

Gorbachev would talk in broken English about how he saw the world. He mourned the fact that governments had not worked harder to foster cooperation between nations. He was convinced that peace and prosperity—especially for the undeveloped countries of the world—were still viable possibilities, but he was not naive about the amount of hard work, trust, and courage required to make it so.

He was honest about the past, never seeking to ignore or avoid it. He would talk about the century of communist rule with real humility and the animosity that existed between the United States and the Soviet Union with sincere regret. Khrushchev and Kennedy, the Cuban Missile Crisis, the Bay of Pigs invasion—these were all on the table. He was not evasive at all, and in his openness, there was a clear sense that he believed our two countries could still work together.

There are some people in America who believe that the collapse of the Soviet Union was caused by the increase in military spending by the Reagan administration, which the Soviets felt compelled to match. I don't believe that was the primary reason, though economic pressures clearly played their part. I am convinced that the Soviet Union had been in decline for years. The people were hungry—as they often are in communist systems—and there was a naive assumption among the leaders that all they needed was for oil prices to rise and then their problems would be over. That revenue never materialized, and the country's commitment to state control meant that they had done nothing to encourage their millions of individuals to innovate and explore and create business and wealth and progress for themselves.

The free market is the only system that works today. It is the only way to empower individuals to fulfill their potential, and in turn it is the only way to unlock a nation's true potential.

Being in the room with Mikhail Gorbachev, sitting across the table while he talked, I was convinced that if he had stayed in power, the world would have looked very different. If we had worked as hard to restore order and establish democracy in Russia at the end of the Cold War as we did in Germany and Japan after the end of the Second World War, life in Russia would have been fundamentally different, not just for the Russian people but for their neighbors and the rest of the world. We missed our chance, and if there's one lesson that we really ought to learn, it's that chances at genuine, world-changing peace don't come along all too often. When we see them, we need to grab them with both hands.

While the political world was changing in the nineties, my own life was also experiencing a transformation. In 1990, after having discussed it with our four daughters, Kathy and I finally divorced. We had been separated for a long time, and though it left me with strong feelings of sorrow and regret, I knew that it was the right decision at the right time.

I was happy being single and kept myself busy by throwing myself into the cosmetics business with my nephew George. I spent most of my time on weekends with my daughters, visiting them at their schools or vacationing in Greece with them. I had no intention of getting married again. There just didn't seem to be the time.

One weekend in 1995, when Barbara and Jennifer were both studying at the University of Denver, I was traveling to Denver to spend the weekend with them. I had just boarded my first flight in Boston and was watching the last few passengers shuffle down the aisle. Just before the doors were closed, a woman rushed on. She was wearing a nice suit and flashed the attendant a broad smile even though she was clearly flustered from having to run for the plane. I glanced back as she found her seat. It was crowded back there.

I settled into my own seat and started on my paperwork as the plane took off. I was flying a lot in those days and always used the time to read, write, and catch up on all the administrative tasks that seemed to escape my attention when I was down on the ground. I was busy working, my papers spread out over the two empty seats beside me. I wasn't focused on anything else.

"Excuse me? Sir?"

I looked up. It was the woman who had rushed on late. That smile was something else. Suddenly, work didn't seem quite so important.

"Would you mind if I sat in this empty seat here?"

"Of course." I was more than happy to move my papers onto the empty seat between us. "I bought the seat for you anyway."

She smiled at my joke, and we started talking. Her name was Karen, and she had a way of asking questions, then really listening to the answers. I had a lot of conversations with a lot of different people, but that first time talking with Karen was different. She was unique, right from the start.

Our conversation lasted throughout the drinks service, the meal, and the quiet lull that settled on the plane before descent. We talked about business—she worked for one of the big Boston banks—and family. She didn't have kids but was close to her parents and brothers.

"I'm heading to Florida today," she said. "It's my father's name day."

"What's his name?"

"Evangelos."

I was intrigued. "Are you Greek?"

"My parents are from Albania."

I smiled. "You know that used to be part of Greece, don't you?"

The conversation continued until we landed in Cincinnati. I didn't do any work at all, instead keeping track of the conversation and all the things she said that I liked: her love of family, the fact that she didn't have kids of her own, and our shared heritage. In the end we exchanged numbers and agreed to meet up some time when we were both back in Boston.

Karen and I became good friends. The more time we spent together, the more we liked each other. We were friends first, then dated for five years. She was wonderful with my girls and their families, as well as with my nephew George and his family. We finally decided to get married in 2000.

My family in Greece loves Karen more than they love me. In every communication I have with my family in Greece, they always ask for Karen and say to make sure to give her their love, and when she talks to them in her limited Greek, they are so excited to hear her voice. She has always been supportive of my business.

---

Meanwhile, there was another major change taking place in the world, this time in the world of manufacturing. Suddenly, everybody appeared to be looking for an LCC—a low-cost country—where they could move their manufacturing to in an effort to be more cost efficient. We were doing a lot of business with Motorola at the time, and they were encouraging us to set up a factory either in China or Mexico, and occasionally they demanded it. I didn't think much of the idea myself but felt that I owed it to them to at least take their request seriously and go see for myself what working with these LCCs might be like.

I flew to Hong Kong in July 1996, then traveled with a few colleagues by train into mainland China. It was my first time there, and my initial impressions were surprisingly positive. The trains ran efficiently, the business contacts who were hosting us were friendly and polite, and the hotel they took us to would not have been out of place in many Western nations. I was ready to be impressed.

The next day we were taken to visit several manufacturing companies. Two things struck me right away.

First, it was the people. I'd heard that China routinely migrated people from rural areas to urban centers so they could staff the factories. I wasn't able to talk to any of the workers and ask them about their lives, but I could see the housing next to the factories—amounting to little more than barracks—in every factory that we visited. It didn't reflect the way that I always thought staff should be treated.

The other thing I noticed was far more positive—at least from a Chinese perspective. We were taken to look at a lot of technical factories that made tools for the plastics businesses. In many of them I saw whole factories filled with engineers. At home, we never had engineers on the factory floor but machine operators instead. The difference was remarkable, with the Chinese engineers able to put out work that adhered to a far higher technical standard than what we would expect in the West.

I left China feeling impressed by their technical efficiency, but instead of wanting to move business overseas, it occurred to me that it would be much better to encourage a far greater scale of vocational training at home. It is a sad truth that our education system does not do nearly enough to encourage or incentivize young men and women to move toward engineering. Why we are so inept at this I don't know.

No country can thrive without a manufacturing base, and if there's one thing that manufacturing relies upon, it is a skilled, well-educated technical workforce.

I also left feeling uneasy about the social conditions in China. It wasn't just the policy of relocating workers hours and hours away from their family homes, accommodating them in barracks, and making it almost impossible for them to travel back home to see their family—often their young children—except for a couple of times each year. I also did not like the way that every time we moved from one city to another, we had to show our papers. Freedom of movement is something that we take for granted in the West. To live without it is very difficult.

In the end we did not partner with any Chinese companies, though we did source some of our tools from them. Today, a quarter century later, we are still working with some Chinese toolmakers but have resisted the trend to ship our production at scale off to one LCC or another.

In that time, the true cost of shifting our manufacturing to China has become apparent. The theft of our intellectual property and patents, the drain in our talent, and the undermining of our own products has harmed us. We might have saved some money, but the true cost has been great.

LCCs seemed like the answer back in the nineties, but it is clear now that they are not the great hope of the future. They come with inherent transportation problems, which add expense, take time, and introduce environmental pollution into the mix. COVID-19 left us exposed to the problems of offshore manufacturing, with so many companies struggling to source their products when the world was shut down. I don't think that LCCs are the answer to all our problems, and I have not given up faith in domestic manufacturing. The costs may be slightly higher but not when we take into account the benefits to the wider economy of having a thriving manufacturing industry at home.

I would like to see our government commit to reshoring, to bringing back our manufacturing from across the Pacific, and to building up the manufacturing industry both at home (especially for medical and other high-value sectors) and to the south. If we were able to pour the right level of investment into developing a high-speed rail network for a freight train that ran from Canada down through Central and into South America, we could protect our own manufacturing industry from supply disruption, reduce costs, protect our intellectual property, reduce the environmental impact of trade, and go a long way toward mitigating the factors that push so many illegal migrants north.

———————

By the time my thoughts on China had clarified and my ideas about reshoring were beginning to take shape, the whole world changed. The events of 9/11 propelled us into a new era of political and economic chaos. Businesses that had been thriving for years suddenly struggled, and for a period it was even difficult to collect receivables. On the day before Thanksgiving, for instance, I had to call the president of a Fortune 500 company that owed us millions of dollars and threaten to put a lien on their facilities in Andover, Massachusetts, if they didn't pay off their debt to us. I'd waited as long as I could, but I reached my limit. Unless he paid, the repercussions for my business were going to be significant.

Our business growth had been steady since our move to Reading, and I had acquired businesses and opened three other plants. But 9/11 unsettled the manufacturing and high-tech industry. I watched the numbers carefully. I could see that business was shrinking and that unless things turned around, we would be in trouble. There were four hundred and fifty people working across my companies, and I didn't want to lose a single one of them, but revenue was sinking lower and lower with every passing quarter.

I started spending my reserves, depleting them month by month. I hoped that things would change, but hope wasn't much use when there was no money coming in. Eventually, with my reserves dropping to perilous levels, I ended up divesting some real estate and consolidating the four different plants into one in Hudson, Massachusetts. It meant losing some staff, which I hated doing, but by then the bigger picture was all that mattered: if we were going to survive, we could only do so if we were smaller.

———————

After 9/11, as we entered what we came to know as the War on Terror, I watched the news like everybody else—perplexed and bewildered by this strange new world. I understood the rage and sorrow and the desire to kill Osama bin Laden, but as we invaded Afghanistan and saw vast numbers of troops die at the hands of an enemy we were struggling to locate, I was unable to make sense of it all. And as the years inched by and the war continued—expanding into Iraq—that feeling of confusion only got worse.

Those cast-iron assurances from our leaders that Saddam Hussein had weapons of mass destruction turned out to be false, leading many of us to mistrust our government. The suffering and collateral damage endured by innocent civilians rose to shocking levels, leading many to question whether we really were doing any good over there. There was torture and corruption, and there was talk of whether this was all about oil and profit. For all those questions, there were too few clear answers.

As the twenty-first century screamed through its first two decades, our news was constantly filled with stories from the Middle East. There was ISIS, Iran's nuclear program, the brutal oppression of the Syrian people by Assad. The whole region seemed to be spiraling out of control. I wondered whether it was always destined to be that way.

Gorbachev was still alive when the War on Terror erupted, but by then his voice and influence had faded. We needed leaders like him, and we still do today. We need leaders who are bold and brave, courageous to the point of being willing to sacrifice not just their careers but their lives. We need leaders who are able to take a long, objective look at the country they love to honestly appraise her mistakes but also be willing—and able—to devise a credible plan to fully unleash her potential. We need leaders committed to genuine reform, bold thinking, openness, honesty, and truth.

We need leaders like this and not just a few of them. We need them all over, in every city and country. Just as the Chinese have invested in their engineers, training them in vast numbers, we need to find a way to train the quality and quantity of leaders that we need today. If we don't, I fear that we'll be shackling ourselves to a future that is a pale imitation of what it could be.

CHAPTER SIXTEEN

# WHEN YOU GIVE, YOU RECEIVE

As I look back now on it now, the summer evening that I spent in New York City twenty-one years ago seems even more significant today than it did then. It was a fairly typical Monday in 2001, but it was just 113 days before the attackers would make the city one of their targets. Four months before everything changed. Today, it seems almost unimaginable to have been there, looking back across the Hudson at the familiar outline of the World Trade Center and be so blissfully unaware of the carnage to come. How could normal life have carried on that summer, when such evil plans were being laid? But we were all innocent then. So much of life before 9/11 seems to belong to a different era altogether.

And yet my memories of what happened on May 21, 2001, are not just influenced by what would eventually happen in the city. My memories are also soaked through with the deep joy and gratitude that I experienced that day. For that was the day that I was awarded the Ellis Island Medal of Honor.

In a lifetime full of wonderful memories and incredible opportunities, it was a day to treasure every moment.

---

I was receiving the award because of my good citizenship, my support of our citizens and the country, and my philanthropy in America. But the story of my giving started years before, even as far back as my earliest days in the village, when we would join with our neighbors to harvest whatever crop was ready. It was through those long days that I learned about the value, as well as the cost, of being generous with what you had. Our backs ached and our fingers cramped as we worked hour after hour, but our hearts were full and our smiles wide as we received each other's gratitude and encouragement.

In giving of our time and effort, we weren't just storing up credit for the day when we would need help to harvest our own crops or paying off a debt we owed for labor already given. We were connected to each other, enjoying the riches of community at its best. We were laughing and joking and learning new skills and teaching old ones. We were giving and receiving, trading in something as simple and basic as sweat, but that had a greater value than gold. On the days when we were helping others, we were showing our neighbors that their welfare mattered to us. On the days when we were the ones being helped, we were being affirmed and loved. Both were a privilege. Both left a deep impression on me.

As I grew up, I leaned toward those nurturing communities like a sunflower reaches toward the sky. I found them

George E. Danis

everywhere I looked: among the crew of *The Atlantic*, waiting for me on the dock in Oakland, in the communities of fellow Greeks in Chicago, Philadelphia, and Boston. We didn't pick olives or plow fields, but the spirit in which they operated was the same. They invited me in to share what they had and valued what I could contribute. In this way, I learned to see that generosity is not an optional extra to be adopted or rejected according to personal taste. I came to see generosity as one of the true essentials for a satisfying life.

As my time in politics came to an end, I began to realize that I had grown a little tired of all the upheaval that goes along with being involved in a campaign. I had also been up close to enough successful politicians to know that many of them will say one thing to get elected and do another thing entirely once in office. It's not always their fault, and all the people I worked with had high standards of personal integrity, but there's a reality to political life that makes compromise essential to survival. The special interests, the party politics, the ideological shifts all add up and exert the kind of pressure that is impossible to resist. Sadly, there's a lot of truth in the old saying that politicians campaign in poetry but govern in prose.

Once I accepted this, I was determined to look around for other ways in which I could make a difference in the lives of our citizens. My eyes settled on the church and the education system. In Boston I connected with the Hellenic College and Holy Cross Greek Orthodox School of Theology, taking on a role as a member of the Board of Trustees. I worked with many of my friends in the Greek community to put on many fundraisers, including sponsoring the first golf tournament in 1996, which has continued to this day with my full support. I also accepted the invitation of a friend to join the Board of Overseers at Northeastern University, traveling with them to Greece in 2006 to expand collaborations with leading academic institutions in Athens.

That was not the only thing. I also continued to be very active with the churches around Boston, funding many of their programs that helped grow the community, especially when younger generations benefited. In addition, I have been supporting the Metropolis of Boston—a program that houses relatives of people coming from overseas for medical procedures—and one of its homes called Philoxenia House. I have been funding a youth Metropolis camp in New Hampshire and did what I could back in Greece as well. I strove to be a good citizen of my hometown, responding to whatever requests I received, and in the late 1980s I was able to gift the hospital in Karystos their first X-ray machine. This year I've been purchasing several pieces of cardiac diagnostic equipment as well as equipment and systems to digitize all the patient records for this hospital.

Back in the United States, I was a cofounder and have continued to support the Hellenic Nursing and Rehabilitation Center in Canton, Massachusetts. In Watertown, Massachusetts, I started hosting annual Thanksgiving dinners for senior citizens for the last forty years and extended the program to support the community in Hudson.

Over the years, I learned a lot about giving from my parents—during the German occupation and depression that followed for many years. But one of the most important lessons is the simplest of all: if you can afford to give, then give. You need to be careful and thorough and ensure that the nonprofit, the project, or the person that you are considering funding is viable and able to deliver what it's promising. But that's often not too hard to figure out. And if you do find something that you're not sure about, then move on and find something else that you do like the look of. The plain truth today is that there are many, many opportunities to give. If you've got the ability to do so, then why wouldn't you?

There's no shame in admitting that giving is a two-way street. Being generous is personally rewarding but not because of the boost to your reputation or ego. Being generous draws you into a deeper connection with others. Generosity connects you with people, and that connection has value. Whether we're seeing people enjoying a free meal, knowing that a difficult period of someone's life has been made just a little bit easier, or watching a person's whole future transforming because of an opportunity you've helped them access, all of this can—and should—leave us smiling. It is good to give because it is good to be able to affirm to others that they matter.

I came to see that generosity is not limited to philanthropy. I once acquired a company that was heading for bankruptcy. There was a very real risk that all 150 of the workforce would lose their jobs. To be able to take that company and turn it around in less than a year, giving those employees economic security—and better compensation—gave me the same feeling of satisfaction that I experienced when signing checks for the latest church initiative to benefit others.

Another time I merged two companies and promoted the administrator to be the overall plant manager. I love moving people into management positions, especially when they've grown used to the assumption that they're not management material. Empowering and rewarding people is one of the biggest rewards out there.

While I am a strong advocate of philanthropy, there are times when it gives me pause. Recently, I was reading about how a certain founder of a Fortune 500 company had been complaining that people are not willing to work anymore. He announced his intention to take his billions (which he has amassed, no doubt, thanks to the hard work of a lot of ordinary Americans), and channel them, tax-free, into a charitable foundation that supports his pet projects. Of course, he has the right to do what he wants with his money, even if it means benefiting from a faulty tax system that our political leaders have failed to fix. The question for me is, how is this helping to create a level playing field? How is it right that the profits generated by all those hardworking employees end up being the plaything of one man?

I am on the side of the low earners who are trying to save money for their children's college education—but who must pay their taxes first. Tax-free foundations for billionaires benefit the billionaires, but surely we can find a better way to spread the benefits wider.

We must challenge our elected officials to level the playing field and treat all people with equality and dignity.

———————

After years of living the way my parents and community taught me, I was invited to New York to receive the award. Being in New York that May evening was special. I'd received rewards from various bodies already, and I appreciated every one of them—accepting them with the same warmth and gratitude with which they had been given. But there was something about the Ellis Island Medal of Honor that made the day feel completely different from any other.

Each year, recipients are selected from those American citizens who exemplify a life dedicated to community service. They are the people who preserve and celebrate the history, traditions, and values of their ancestry while exemplifying the values of the American dream and way of life and who are dedicated to creating a better world for us all. Over the years the award has honored everyone from Frank Sinatra to Muhammad Ali, from Elie Wiesel to Joe DiMaggio. It has honored presidents, celebrities, and Nobel Prize winners. To be one of the winners celebrated each year is an honor that is hard to compare.

Karen and I had already attended a reception the night before that was hosted by a Greek organization in the city, but the dinner at the award itself left me a little awestruck. The event venue was perfect, with one of the large Ellis Island halls full of recipients and their families. Everyone was wearing fine gowns, immaculate tuxes, and easy smiles. Karen and I had been married a little more than a year, and it was extra special to share my table with her, Stella and Marina, and their husbands. The whole family couldn't be there, but I felt loved and supported in ways that only made my smile brighter.

Looking around at my fellow awardees that night was a little like being in a dream—a dream made up of so many immigrants. There was Mayor Rudy Giuliani (Italian); internationally acclaimed opera singer Renée Fleming (Czech, Scottish, Irish); the mystery author Mary Higgins Clark (Irish); the actor best known as Klinger on the television show *M*A*S*H*, Jamie Farr (Lebanese); and baseball legend Yogi Berra (another Italian). Of the 138 honorees that night, it felt like almost half were immigrants. Later, I discovered that eighteen of them were Greek-American.

Between the conversation and the moments of staring around the room, I found myself thinking about the significance of being there—on Ellis Island itself—not just for me, but for Karen and the girls. For an immigrant like me, and with Karen being the daughter of an immigrant, the Statue of Liberty that we had passed by as we took the ferry from Battery Park had tremendous significance. What clearer symbol could there be of the promise of America? What other sight so powerfully illustrates the hope that the country offers to those who are searching for a brighter future? What other country would proudly display so open and generous an invitation to those in search of a new home?

For any first- or second-generation immigrant in America, there are few locations more powerful than Liberty Island.

I thought about my Uncle Alex that day, my mother's brother in Philadelphia who took me in when I jumped ship for the second time. He left Greece early in the twentieth century, traveling across the Atlantic by boat just like the millions of others who emigrated at that time. He passed through the halls on Ellis Island, hoping to be allowed in, and made it. Years had passed since he died, but that day, as Karen and I boarded the ferry and made our way across the Hudson River, I felt something of his presence. He made it. He built a good life for himself. He achieved everything in America that he had hoped to accomplish. I was proud of him.

These days we talk a lot about immigration, and most of the time the story is heavily edited to present only the negatives. We hear about us being overrun, about armies and caravans and criminals and smugglers. And yes, there are problems. The system is being mismanaged by our government, and there are communities along the border that have suffered as a result.

But by only revealing one half of the story, we fail to be fully informed. We are unaware of the costs that most migrants have already paid in order to get here. We can't imagine what it must take to be willing to pack up your family, say goodbye to your homeland, and make such a perilous journey in the hopes of building a new life for yourself. For many of us, the thought is just too difficult to comprehend.

Liberty Island reminds us that it has not always been this way in America. We haven't always been so suspicious or closed off. For a period of six decades, twelve million people sailed into New York, disembarked in the shadow of the Statue of Liberty, and were welcomed as citizens. They went on to become our factory workers and engineers, our construction workers and farmers, our nurses and entrepreneurs. They worked for the good of the country, building their own futures here while creating a bright, prosperous future that we all enjoy today. And when the call came, many of them went back across the Atlantic or over the Pacific to fight and die for the very freedom they had risked so much to reach in the first place.

So much has already been written about immigration, but I believe there is real value in sharing these stories. Mine is not unique by any means, and there are plenty of immigrants who have come from harsher backgrounds than mine and built bigger fortunes. Comparing and contrasting misses the point. The real gold in sharing stories about modern-day immigrants is not in the difference but in the similarity. Stories of men and women who took a risk and trusted that it would pay off in America are all echoes of the millions and millions of others who did the same, traveling here even in the years before Ellis Island even existed.

———————

After we had eaten, the atmosphere in the hall shifted. It was time for the awards to be handed out, with nominees brought up a few at a time to wait at the side of the stage before being called up by name.

I received my cue, embraced Karen and the girls, then I left the table.

Time slowed down as I waited and listened to the names being called.

"George Argyros…"

Each winner had a brief summary read out as they walked up to collect their medal. With so many awards to hand out, there would be no opportunity for a speech. No matter. I was delivering it silently in my head anyway.

I was grateful for the love and care shown to me by my parents and brothers. For the nurture of my village. For the people in Athens who helped me, especially Captain Manoli. For the crew of the *Atlantic Sea*. For Vasillis Novas and the good people of Oakland and San Francisco. For Father Metaxas. Mr. and Mrs. Contos. My mother's cousin Alex Paraskos and his whole family, and for Jim Lemonias and his family. For my uncle Alex and his wife Georgia. Michael Dukakis. Senator Ted Kennedy and his brother John, the president who appreciated the value of both immigrants and the contributions that Greece has made to the world.

The list was long, and I could see before me a great crowd of good and kind people who had all extended their friendship to me. Without them and their kindness, I would not have come so far.

"Arthur Cheliotes…"

As well as expressing all this deep gratitude for so many

wonderful people who had helped me, my silent speech contained a word of advice: *don't forget your background.* There, in the hall on Ellis Island that a century earlier had been filled with migrants drawn from all over the world, I wanted people to remember and celebrate the heritage that formed them. For Greeks like me, our legacy of democracy, equality, and freedom still shines a light today.

In today's polarized, politicized world, I urge us all to remember that America's strength has always come from her willingness to take in those in need of refuge and to be shaped by them in turn. We are a light to the world, and the light is made brighter by those we welcome.

"George E. Danis."

As I walked to the front of the stage, I was only vaguely aware of the announcer sharing the few words of biography that tried to sum up my life. I paused before the chairman of the awards committee, and for a brief moment there was silence in the hall.

I bent forward and felt the medal land around my neck.

A quick handshake. A photograph.

Then I was off, back to my table and family. Their smiles and their hugs could have lasted a lifetime.

# FIX THINGS

IT IS EARLY OCTOBER 2022, and the Aegean Sea is still warm enough for me to swim. I'm a little more careful entering the water than I used to be—no more sprinting across the beach, launching myself full-flight, and splashing down as I did when I was a child. But the pleasure I feel as I swim away from the shore is exactly the same as it ever was. I let myself lie back and stare up at the perfectly clear sky. I am held. I am home.

It is here, just a mile or so outside Karystos, that I return to as often as I can each year. My real home is still in Boston, and running the business there keeps me busy. But it is here, with Mili nestling in the hills above, that I feel I truly belong. Here, where evening meals start at ten o'clock and the conversation is a woven tapestry of gossip and laughter, politics, and stories about the people we remember who are no longer with us. Here, where belonging to a community is measured not by your address but by how much of yourself you are prepared to give to others—your laughter, your time, your interest.

This is where I was formed. This is where my heart calls home. This is where my values were forged—especially the most Greek wisdom of all: *pan metron ariston.*

It means *everything in moderation,* and it's a powerful and vital mantra to follow. It helps us to stay physically healthy and avoid gluttony, but it also develops within us a deeply grateful attitude. When you live your life following *pan metron ariston,* you naturally want to give thanks to the source of all this goodness that you taste in moderation, including your citizenship responsibilities and obligations.

Growing up working on the farm, we were very appreciative to the Almighty Creator for our health and the ability to work and survive. My parents and the entire community of seventy families were church-going people, blessed and thankful to God for our survival. I was taught at home to be kind, respectful to all, and very helpful to everyone around me.

My mother always said that I had an angel protecting me, and I have never really doubted it. With all the journeys and challenges that followed, I was always able to survive and make out good.

Today, I am continuing to try to share what I can with others. It makes me very happy to do this, and as long as I can, I will continue promoting unity, gratitude, and a view of people as equal citizens.

Wealth is good, but *pan metron ariston.* It is not good to grow fat or greedy or miserly in your bank balance. Enjoy it in moderation. Be generous. Give it away.

More than two decades have passed since I received the Ellis Island Medal of Honor, and in many ways, there is not much that has changed. I have continued to support the causes that I care about, and I continue to take great joy from seeing my employees receive the best treatment in the business. Maybe I am a bit more direct with people these days than I used to be—I recently tried to bribe some builders working on my house to quit smoking—but little has really changed.

We all went through challenges during those times. When the financial crisis of 2007 and 2008 hit, business became harder than ever. Loans were almost impossible to secure, and many companies faced bankruptcy, especially those who hadn't factored a possible downturn into their forecasts. Some of our customers were in this position, and we had to think creatively in order to do what we could to keep them going. It became clear to me then that most entrepreneurs lack the training to really build an organization long term. The big picture interests many of them so much more than the small. But the small picture matters most of all. How you treat your employees will most likely play a much bigger part in how your business performs than your marketing strategy does. It's the same with social change. If we want to see things improved, progress is most likely going to be won inch by inch, not mile by mile. Person to person, not leader to nation.

My industry has changed a lot over the years.

After the devastation of the U.S. manufacturing base, I started to plan for the future. Today, I remain focused on how we can bring back manufacturing to the United States. We need to make the future more friendly and supportive for business, with more automation and improved quality. The American people have our political leaders to thank for the current climate of chaos, where our manufacturing businesses are routinely given away to the rest of the world through the trade agreements that politicians have negotiated.

Placing manufacturing in countries with no human rights and little care for their citizens, where pay is so low and poverty reigns, has been a disaster. And because of this, our politicians have made it easy for the American people to become dependent on that low-cost labor to supply what we need, without thinking about where these products come from and what these people have endured to manufacture them. This is why I believe our southern neighbors could have benefited if we had moved our manufacturing to the Southern hemisphere and trained and helped people to succeed. We could have made the supply chain more sustainable and more beneficial to all citizens of the Americas and would have also created a new market as people and businesses prospered from our support.

———————

One evening I went with Karen to a dinner party and concert she had set up for the customers of the largest bank in

Boston. I was seated next to the bank's chairman, her boss, and we talked for an hour and a half during dinner, covering many subjects, including the bank's business, expansion, and acquisition of other small banks. On the way home Karen and I talked about the evening, including my conversation with the chairman.

"He'll be fired by the board within a year," I said.

Karen was not happy. I explained my reasoning as best I could—how I sensed that he was desperately trying to cover the fact that he was in way over his head—and the conversation ended.

Six months later he was sacked.

Some of our highest positions are held by people who are simply not competent. The same is true of smaller businesses. There are many out there whose leaders are trying to hide the disaster they have presided over.

In recent years I have found myself being drawn to these companies, looking for ways to help them and prevent them from filing bankruptcy— and save people's jobs—by purchasing them and turning the business around for everybody's benefit.

In 2010 I started to research companies that needed financial help. I found and acquired Res-Tech plastic injection molding out of Clinton, Massachusetts, with plants in Leominster and Peabody, Massachusetts. There were four owners, and it was a difficult time to sustain the company. I worked with the bank and took over the debt with substantial equity of my own.

I presented my plan to the bank, showing how I would turn the company around, and the bank agreed with my plan. Unfortunately, some small business owners don't have the knowledge and never acquire experience during hard times of how to run the company's financial business. Res-Tech had been bleeding for a few years, and they were in serious trouble, even drawing the funding for their last payroll from a closed bank account (the bank clerk did not research the transaction thoroughly enough to know the company had been sold, and he released the funds).

As I arrived at Res-Tech for my first day, my first task was to research and analyze where the losses were coming from. I wanted to find out what was going on in each department and how we could minimize their losses and turn it into profitability. I turned up and was surprised that no one was at their desks. My first reaction was panic, thinking everyone had quit, but I could hear talking in the conference room.

I joined them, sat down, and listened as twelve people spent about twenty minutes talking about things that had no relevance to their problems at all. When the discussion finished, the facilitator told them they were going to have another meeting on Wednesday.

"Well," I said, "let's hold fire on that. I'll let you know if and when the next meeting will take place." I asked the facilitator to remain behind so we could talk.

"I'm the new owner," I said when we were alone. "You and I have not met before, but from now on you need to clear it with me before you gather people together like this to discuss things that have no relevance to their individual departments."

He agreed, and we worked well together from then on.

My next meeting was with the controller, who presented me with a check of $21,000 to sign for credit cards. Every department manager had a credit card, and they were charging their lunches and any other small things they would purchase to the company. This was both a surprise and concern.

"How many cards in total?" I asked.

"Twenty-three," said the controller.

I asked him to go collect them all and bring them to me. When he had them all on his desk, I asked him if he knew the numbers and the banks that they were drawing from. He nodded.

"Great," I said. "One last thing. Do you have a pair of scissors?"

It was his turn to look surprised and concerned.

He pulled a pair of scissors from his desk and handed them over. I started cutting the cards up.

"Smile," I told him when I was nearly done. "We just saved the company $250,000 each year."

That wasn't the end of it. When the suppliers heard about the company's transition, they shipped all the open purchase orders the day before we closed the transaction, at a cost to the company of over $750,000. When I heard about this on my first day, I instructed the purchasing manager to bring in truckers from wherever he could find and ship back the material to the suppliers immediately.

My next meeting was with the plant in Peabody. It was also losing money due to their low sales and the products that they were producing, plus the overhead they were charged. My visit with the lady who served as plant manager was very cordial, and it was clear that she was capable and experienced. As our conversation ended, I asked her if she wanted to buy the company.

"I don't know if I can afford it," she said.

"I'll sell it to you at the price I paid for it."

She thought a while. "Can you wait while I talk with my family?"

I had no choice and told her to let me know whenever she was ready.

The next day, she called me to say that she accepted the offer and would buy the plant in Peabody for $280,000. It was a good deal, as the company was worth almost twice that, but it didn't fit in with our business strategy.

And so, in less than one week, I was able to level the playing field across the business. The losses stopped, and nine months later, at year's end, the company was making double what it had been losing at the same period the year before. The bank was elated with the progress we made.

I continued to search for companies that were losing money, and the next one I found was in Berlin, Connecticut. Tech Atlantic was in the same condition as Res-Tech—the owner was unable to run the company and was losing money—and I acquired it in 2013, happy to be able to save the company and preserve people's jobs. I also helped the landlord by continuing to lease his building rather than leave it empty had the company failed. I promoted the people who were already working to fill different managerial positions and made the administrator the new plant manager. I acquired another company in Connecticut that same year and merged it with Tech Atlantic. Under the new plant manager's leadership, the company is now doing very well, having weathered the storms of COVID-19. In total, over 150 jobs were saved.

One year later I found a company in Lancaster, Pennsylvania. The financial situation was devastating, just like the others. Once more I promoted from within, making one of the production managers the new plant manager.

The next one was in South Bend, Indiana. The company was owned by two people who had almost run it into the ground by low-balling the pricing to get more sales—something that you should never do. When I acquired the company, I found that some of the people had not even been trained. I was able to turn it around, and they are doing a super job with the same people who were there when we acquired the company.

In 2021 I acquired our sixth company. It was in Putnam, Connecticut, and again the financial condition of the company was terrible. Due to the size of the building and sales, I decided to relocate the business to the other four plants. The customers are very pleased, and the team is doing an excellent job managing the new products and increasing the sales.

With all these acquisitions, my goal was to help. I wanted to prevent the calamity of redundancy and create better working conditions for people. I did this because of the values that were sown into me when I was a child. I was taught that every voice matters, every individual is a citizen, and every citizen has a right and a responsibility to do what they can to improve the lives of others.

I want to encourage all of us—whether or not we are business owners or workers—to participate and to be good citizens of our country. I believe that it is especially vital for business leaders to be committed to promoting goodwill and participating in every aspect of our community. We have responsibility toward people, and in many ways, we must be organizers, gathering and resourcing people and equipping them to succeed. It's not such a strange idea, really: the citizens of the United States promoted a community organizer as our forty-fourth president of the United States.

---

In other parts of life, everything has changed. I am no longer just a father to my four daughters. I am a father-in-law to their spouses and *papou* to their nine children. Stella and Edward have two boys, Christopher and William. Christopher worked with me for a while and is now back in school studying for his MBA. William got his master's and is preparing to apply to medical schools.

Barbara and Jon have Theodore and Anna. Theodore just started his freshman year in college, and his sister, Anna, is a junior in high school. Marina and Dean have three daughters: a set of twins, Alexandra and Stephanie, who have both graduated from college. Alex is a teacher, while Stephanie is working in food science. Their third daughter, Katherine, is a freshman in college.

Jennifer just lost her spouse and has adopted two children. Sha'Day is ten years old, and Alan is seven years old. Jennifer works for the school system as a therapist.

All of my daughters are very supportive of each other. It makes my heart smile to see them bring up their children as they do.

The times when all of us are gathered here at the house in Karystos—three generations as well as my brother Polychronis, his two sons, Xristos and Panagiotis, and his daughter Stella; Evangelos's widow, Fini, and their daughter Mary; her husband, Dimitri, and their son, Jason; and my other brother, Alexandros, his wife, Maria, and their son, Evangelos—are some of the most precious memories of each year.

I am not only a father or grandfather. Like everyone else, I am a citizen of America and the world. The human experience will always be the foundation of the future, and we will never graduate from it.

For me, it is clear that the foundations of society go back to my ancient countrymen. The Western world that cherishes democracy was born and nurtured through our Greek ancestors. Throughout my life I have done everything in my power to stay true to those core values of my heritage: intellectual curiosity; a desire to live in harmony and respect all, including our big home, the planet, with its abundant natural world; a commitment to harmony with others; and an unshakeable belief in the power of the citizen.

We need those strong foundations today, especially as so much of the world has changed in recent decades and even in recent years. The climate emergency is fiercer, political division appears wider, and after COVID-19, prosperity and stability seem further away than before. The playing field is far from level, and the sense of citizenship is low. We are living in a world of grown-up problems, but too many politicians are capable of offering only playground solutions in a polarized manner.

Today, like every country on the planet, we are still living with the effects of COVID-19, but our response is misguided. We have lost a significant portion of our labor force and are struggling to produce products we need. Prices are rising and inflation is going up. The Federal Reserve Board is trying to offset that by increasing interest rates, all of which means that those with the least end up feeling the most financial pain. Seven and eight percent interest rates make loans unaffordable for many businesses and would-be homeowners. We're heading for another crisis of bankruptcies and need to be very careful as citizens about how we approach this next season. We need to control our spending, period.

I would like to see a change in the approach to government funding, but I doubt it will happen of its own accord. Politicians aren't going to voluntarily put themselves under more scrutiny, and they're unlikely to stop trying to win our affection with giveaways anytime soon. So what we need to do as members of the public is pressure our leaders to give a full and detailed account of how each new program will be funded. We need to be rigorous and demanding, and we can't rest until we have created a culture where our politicians treat us less like tired and hungry children and more like responsible, analytical adults. After all, they work for us.

Some people feel powerless as individuals. It shouldn't be that way, and if ever I needed a reminder of the power of an individual to impact someone else's life, I got it in 2016. I applied for a gun license and went to my local police station to get fingerprinted. A week later I got a call from the chief of police.

"George? Something came up with your prints."

"That's funny, Chief."

"No, I'm not joking. It says here that you're a fugitive. Something about not leaving the country when you were supposed to back in 1957. Do you know anything about that?"

I took a breath, tried to keep calm, and told him that what I knew was that I had complied exactly with the order I had been given to leave the country by Senator John F. Kennedy. I had been careful to travel down to New York, where I was sure to have my papers stamped so that my exit would be recorded. "This is a mistake, Chief. Someone must have messed up. It can't be a big deal. I've been a citizen for decades. I've got my passport and everything."

"Well, it says here that I could have you arrested."

I could feel the walls closing in.

The chief was kind, though, and he had no intention of arresting me. I hired an attorney, filed a Freedom of Information request for my exit paperwork, and waited for the reply.

When the papers came, it was a relief. There, third page from the top, was the form correctly filled out that confirmed I had left the country legally within the time frame that I was given. Somewhere along the line, someone just didn't do their job properly.

The problem was eventually solved, and my license was granted, but the fact remained that someone had messed up. If I hadn't been able to afford an attorney or didn't already have the trust of my local chief of police, the outcome for me could have been very different. This is an example of how our government institutions are not committed to serving their citizens and doing their jobs correctly, just like my friend who has had similar problems with the IRS. It is up to us to demand a more perfect union to service quality to their citizens.

---

Citizenship is not a one-way transaction. Citizenship brings with it so many benefits, but it also confers certain responsibilities. If we want to belong to a democratically run country and be protected by its laws and enjoy its freedoms, then it seems to me that the most basic requirement is that we know how our government works. We need to be informed of the way things work and become engaged in the effort to meet our country's needs. It is not enough to take what we want, gripe about what is bad, and offer nothing of ourselves.

Citizenship doesn't work that way. Citizenship requires participation. Citizenship happens only when you and I show up.

Here's where I think we can make a change: we should make it easier for our citizens to vote. After all, how hard can it be? As soon as we're born, we have a social security number, and as soon as we start working, we're taxed. Why can't the government put as much effort into collecting our votes as it does into collecting our taxes?

———————

Recently, a friend of mine has been in conflict with our U.S. government and the IRS. He pays quarterly estimated taxes as normal in advance of the ensuing year, and as a good, law-abiding citizen, and—because of his CPA's advice—he mistakenly overpaid in taxes. So when he filed his tax returns, he had a refund due, but it has taken him numerous video conference calls to try to get his refund. It has now been over three and a half months, and the IRS continues delaying the process. They keep repeating their requests to validate who the person looking for the refund is. His CPA said it is the way the government works, that they only know how to take. Unfortunately, we the people have allowed the government and their agencies to mishandle the citizens and give us a hard time about our rights. They don't care to serve the citizens of the country that they work for.

We need to demand the service that we require and deserve. The government collects taxes, takes our money—and God knows how or where they are spending it around the world—while our own citizens (including most of our veterans who fought the wars to protect and defend our freedom) are not being taking care of. Many water systems in U.S. cities are a dismal failure, the infrastructure is deteriorating, an adult education system is missing, and many services have been inadequate. If we want change, we must demand it.

We, the citizens, need to demand that our leaders be more accountable when they spend our tax dollars with no results. We chase wars overseas while at home our problems increase. Our citizens lack access to clean, safe drinking water, veterans are struggling to cope, many of our people are suffering greatly, and yet some politicians appear to care more about taking credit for some overseas intervention than about leveling the domestic playing field.

The answer is simple. The answer is clear. The answer is you, the citizens that make up this country.

I urge you to act. I urge you to take note of the things that bother you—whether it's the climate, the culture, or the way our country is approaching any of the many issues that need addressing—and act. Be curious about how things can be improved. Be restless until you see change. And be prepared to use some of the time, talent, and resources at your disposal to act.

That curiosity and restlessness was a part of my character from a young age, and it got me into plenty of trouble. But it got me into so much more that was good. Curiosity and restlessness have been two of my most important assets since

I left home more than seventy years ago. They still serve me well today.

This is what I want to say to you: fix things. I want you to fix things with your own hands. Fix things with your own sweat. Fix things with other people at your side, working in tandem with your community—both alongside those whom you find easy to be with and with others who require more of your patience. Don't be an extremist. It will not work for a sustainable future.

Fix things.

Because the world needs people that are not content to be spectators. The world needs people who are prepared to act. Just as it always has done.

# ACKNOWLEDGMENTS

A long life like mine weaves together many threads, and as I look back on the rich tapestry of my experience, I owe a debt of gratitude to a great many, many people. Some are still with us and able to read these words; others have since departed. All of them have shaped me.

From the years growing up in Greece I am grateful to the following people that were part of my life:

Our neighbors next door, the Mperetis family. Vangelis was my age and we always played together, his whole family keeping us out of trouble and safe. There was the Thomas family (Mitsouliou), the Thepas family, and the Sarlanis family. There was a whole neighborhood around us and their wisdom, their values, and their view of life itself made me into the citizen I am today.

Dr. Panagiotou inspired me to donate the first X-ray machine to the hospital in Karystos, Evia, Greece.

My dear friend John and I grew up in Milos. While I settled in the U.S., he continued his career at sea. Sadly, his ship went down in the South China Sea. May his memory be eternal.

My dear friend Vangelis Thomas (Kokinos) arrived in Boston illegally and I got him a job at Wilson's Diner in Waltham, Massachusetts. Later he was deported back to Greece, and we were friends for life. He is no longer with us. May his memory be eternal.

Throughout my childhood, America was always my chosen destination. From the moment I arrived I felt the warmth, love, and encouragement of so many people:

My cousin Alex Paraskos picked me up at the train station in Boston, introduced me to his family. Alex was always there whenever I needed help or advice, and his brothers Demetrios and Vangelis were big supporters.

I am grateful for my dearest friend, confidante, and supporter Jim Lemonias. His family was like my second family in Watertown! My dearest friend Sia Lemonias was always keeping me company introducing me to many of her friends.

Louis Contos (my first boss) and his lovely wife Amersouda took me to their home when I was working for them at Town Diner in Watertown. Louis's son George and his wife Thioni invited me to my first Christmas party in the USA.

Eva Kostopoulos, it has been etched on my memory, the first Christmas gift I received from Eva. Thank you very much and may her memory be eternal!

To the Metropoulos family, from Arlington Street, Watertown. You have always been so kind to me. I have such fond memories in my Greek neighborhood entertaining ourselves and playing soccer with Dean and his sister Georgia. Thank you for being such a good friend.

My spiritual leader, Father Emanual Metaxas hosted me on the first Sunday dinner at his home with his family! May his memory be eternal.

After I became a U.S. citizen, the support, advice, help, recognition, respect, and admiration came from every Greek American to whom I remain humbly grateful. To name but a few:

Charlie Johnson, Attorney, my advisor in legal matters.

My dear friend Peter Agris, publisher of *Hellenic Chronicle.*

Paul Liakos, Chief Justice of the Massachusetts Supreme Court.

My dear friend Dr. Nick Zervas, who always kept me healthy.

Orestis Demetriades, whenever I needed help with the community, Orestis was the one I went to. Thank you very much, may your memory be eternal.

My dear friend Arthur Koumantzelis, Managing Director of Arthur Young, with his lovely wife Vaia, always there for me, and the best man at our wedding.

Telemachus Demoulas, owner of Market Basket supermarkets, a great advisor.

Chris Kokinas, Table Talk Pie always invited me to play golf.

My good friend, Angelos Skangas, owner of West Lynn Creamery.

George D. Behrakis, pharmaceutical manufacturer and philanthropist.

My good friend Arthur Anton, owner of Anton Cleaners.

The Pappas family were there for me in all the Greek events.

My dear friend Bill Markos used to call me to invite me to his parties.

My dear friend Nick Lazares helped me, and we went sailing together many times.

I have learned so much from Arthur T. Demoulas. He is one friend who I would feel so comfortable with listening to his wisdom, philosophy, and love of humanity.

My dearest friend Xristos Tsagganis and I traveled together often, and he would panic if he thought he forgot his blood pressure pills and then found them in his pocket!

My good friends Bill and Teddie Kapos take time to visit us in Karystos and we always love to be together and go to the buzoukia (the Greek night clubs). Thank you, Billy and Teddie!

His Eminence, Metropolitan Methodios, my spiritual leader, works tirelessly to serve all in the Greek community. Thank you very much your Eminence, may God keep your health and energy to continue his work!

My very good friend John Karykas from New York traveled in Greece and around New England skiing.

My friend Gus Saravanos would meet in New York every time I would go there, and moved to Florida.

Stamatis Astra keeps my abreast of the Greek community's information, and always calls me to wish me well!

A special friend, T A Demoulas. I will never forget his calls during the pandemic asking what we needed to bring to our home. Thank you very much young man, you are the greatest!

Great friends! Without them I would have gotten lost in this great country of ours!

As a businessman, my very first steps were assisted by many people, like Anna Cagos (godmother to my daughter, Barbara). Anna loaned me $600 to purchase a home for an investment, which eventually yielded the money that I used to start my career in business. My boss, Charlie at McNabb Engineering, gave me a job, then when he had to lay me off, found me another job which paid even more! As I gained experience in business, I continued to benefit from the wisdom and support of many wonderful people, like my mentor Bernie Creighton. His sage advice and wisdom helped me enormously.

To these people and more I owe so much gratitude. Their help, advice, respect, support, acknowledgment, and admiration have been vital in guiding my journey. These great people were, and still are, my treasure and I am indebted to them with my greatest appreciation!

My involvement with politics brought me into contact with yet more people to whom I am grateful today:

Governor Michael Dukakis made possible my first political involvement. Senator Edward Kennedy was my inspiration in trying to level the playing field. Senator Paul Tsongas, a very forward thinker, reminded the Democrats you need to make the pie before you try to divide it.

Writing this book would not have been possible without the help of Paul Crochiere, and to his wife Nancy, who was kind enough to direct me to her friend Holly who did a beautiful job editing. Dan, Nate, and Will at Gotham, Lauren Magnussen at Amplify, and my writer, Craig Borlase. Holly Robinson offered invaluable editorial advice, and to all of you I say thank you very much!

My biggest supporters in my business career have been four women. In my earlier years it was Jane Argento, then after Jane retired it was Jeannie, and now it is the indispensable Jody Heyward. I would never have succeeded without their support and advice every business day! Another member of our team, our financial expert Jacqui Nielsen, has kept my business finances in perfect order and keeps everyone in line! I want to thank them very much for all they have done for me and my family! I had the pleasure to work with a great friend, Richard McKenney, for over 40 years. An Irish and a Greek together! And John Giannakouras, who worked with me for over 25 years. Jamie Shaw, one of my right-hand men who has been traveling down from Maine every day for over 25 years to keep my properties in good order! Thank you very much!

Professor Petros Vamvakas, my partner on my podcast. I met him when he was 14 years old and we continue to discuss democracy and citizenship.

Professor Constantine Arvanitopoulos from the Fletcher School, a great friend and my podcast partner on democracy and citizenship.

Most of all, I am grateful to my family in Greece. To my brothers Vangellis, Polychroni, Alexandros, and to my wonderful sisters-in-law, Fini, Pagona, and Maria! All three brothers were my constant companions, friends, advisors, and sometimes when required, disciplinarians. I love you all very much!

To my beloved nephew George, who immigrated to the United States, was like the son I never had, the best friend, advisor, and a sounding board to me and to the whole family. We lost George and we continue to miss him. May his memory be eternal.

To my wonderful niece Mary Polychroniou and her family. Mary is my advisor, confidante, and protector for all my business endeavors in Greece.

To my nephew Xristos, who has worked with me on some Greek business ventures.

Last but not least, an amazing young man that I met in 2017 while building the house in Greece. With his outstanding character, he has been my right-hand man on every endeavor, all over Greece. Thank you very much, Panagiotis.

I want to thank my four amazing daughters, Stella, Barbara, Marina, and Jennifer, and to their spouses, Ed, Jon, and Dean, and their nine children, my grandchildren: Christopher, Alexandra, Stephanie, William, Theodore, Katherine, Anna, Sha'Day, and Alan, who have been my life and my inspiration!

Finally, to my lovely wife Karen. Thank you for your unconditional support, advice, and love, and for putting up with all my spontaneous and spur-of-the-moment endeavors and decisions throughout my life, including my involvement with political affairs, as I always talk about how we can FIX the world issues. I am grateful to you for always supporting me and agreeing to follow me, as I am always on the move!

George E. Danis
Boston, Massachusetts
December 2023

# ABOUT THE AUTHOR

George E. Danis is a successful businessman, organizer, entrepreneur, and philanthropist. Born into poverty in rural Greece, George entered the U.S. as an illegal immigrant, yet decades later was awarded the Ellis Island Medal of Honor in recognition of his philanthropic endeavors and promotion of democracy. Highly active in politics for four decades, George was a fundraiser, advocate, and advisor to governors, senators, and presidential candidates. Today he divides his time between Boston, Massachusetts, and his childhood town of Karystos, Greece. He is married to his wife, Karen, has four children, and nine grandchildren.